Off-Road Emergency Repair and Survival

D0027016

OFF-ROAD EMERGENCY REPAIR AND SURVIVAL

James Ristow

John Muir Publications
Santa Fe, New Mexico

John Muir Publications, P.O. Box 613,
Santa Fe, NM 87504

First Edition. First printing

Library of Congress Cataloging-in-Publication Data

Ristow,James,1951-
    Off-road emergency repair and survival/James Ristow.—1st ed.
       p.   cm.
    Includes index.
    ISBN 0-945465-26-2
    1. All terrain vehicles—Maintenance and repair—Handbooks,
manuals,etc. I. Title.
TL235.6.R57 1989
629.28'7042—dc20   88-43529
                                     CIP

Distributed to the book trade by:
W.W. Norton & Company, Inc.
New York, New York

Typeface: Bookman
Designer: Carolyn Ogden

Notice to Readers

The temporary repair methods described in this book will allow you to drive your vehicle but may reduce its mechanical performance.

Anyone who continues to drive a temporarily repaired vehicle after reaching a place where permanent repairs can be made, drives a temporarily repaired vehicle at high speeds, or attempts dangerous terrain with a poorly operating vehicle may cause damage to the vehicle or injury to passengers.

Repair and survival suggestions in this book are intended only as alternatives that may help prevent injury or towing expense due to stranding. The decision to use any method suggested in this book is understood to be at the vehicle owner's discretion without guarantee of success or safety.

All recommended repairs are believed to be safe for both passengers and vehicle if used at slow off-road speeds under reasonable operating conditions.

The author and publisher accept no liability for injuries to persons or damage to property as a result of accidents, mishaps, or exposure to natural elements that readers of this book may experience.

Contents

Introduction   1
   RESPONSIBILITY OF OWNER   3
   HOW TO USE THIS MANUAL   5
   TOOLS, SUPPLIES, EQUIPMENT   9

Part I. Diagnosis and Repair
  1 Engine Turns Over But
    Fails to Start   19
   TESTING IGNITION   20
   NO SPARK FROM PLUG WIRES   23
   NO SPARK FROM COIL WIRE   27
   STATIC IGNITION TIMING   38
   FUEL SYSTEM   41
  2 Engine Does Not Turn Over   51
   TEST THE BATTERY CHARGE   52
   STARTER CLICKS WHEN KEY
    IS TURNED   53
   NO SOUND WHEN KEY IS TURNED   55
   STARTER SPINS FREE   59
   STARTER CHATTERS OR GRINDS   60
   BAD STARTER MOTOR   63
  3 Battery Not Charging   65
   NO CHARGING OR DISCHARGE AT IDLE   66
   BATTERY DRAINS OR SEEMS LOW
    AFTER PARKING   69
  4 Engine Overheating   72
   FLUID LOSS FROM COOLING SYSTEM   72
   NO SIGN OF FLUID LOSS   74
  5 Low Oil Pressure   83
   UNUSUAL OIL CONSUMPTION   85
   ENGINE OIL PAN PUNCTURES   85
   OIL LEVEL NORMAL   86

6 Brake Failure 87

7 Flat Tires 90

    PUNCTURES 90

    TORN VALVE STEMS 92

    JACKING VEHICLE 93

8 Driveline Failure 97

    ENGINE RUNS, VEHICLE FAILS
      TO MOVE 98

    CLUTCH FAILS TO DISENGAGE 102

Part II. Outdoor Skills and Survival

9 Getting Stuck and Unstuck 107

10 First Aid 115

    EXPOSURE 115

    POISONOUS BITES 120

11 Survival 129

    EVALUATING YOUR SITUATION 129

    ATTRACTING HELP 130

    PICKING YOUR ROUTE 131

    GOING FOR HELP 134

    WATER 135

    SHELTER 139

    CLOTHING 143

12 The Environment 146

13 A True Experience 153

Index 163

Introduction

An old sailor once said, "The sailor that ain't run aground, ain't sailed too far." The same is true of land travel. Eventually, every motorist will find himself stranded due to unforeseen mechanical failure. It is inevitable.

To most people, the amount of inconvenience caused by a mechanical failure is directly proportional to the vehicle's distance from the nearest service station. But each year, millions of people are drawn to wilderness areas where there are no services, and vehicles are subjected to grueling off-pavement punishment. Most people depend entirely on the reliability of their vehicles to deliver them safely back to civilization.

A mechanical failure that diverts time from planned activity, causing delay and unnecessary expense, is bad enough, but for individuals who are attracted by the solitude of the outdoors, there is greater risk. Even in rough terrain, a vehicle will travel four or more times faster than walking. A breakdown in the middle of nowhere can strand off-roaders days from help. With a bit of bad luck, the desire to be alone can turn into a dangerous survival situation.

Every experienced off-roader has found himself "beached" at one time or another. Some off-roaders join clubs that hold group outings, and others only drive frequently traversed roads so they are assured of being able to stop a "good samaritan."

It is not always practical to caravan, and everyone is tempted to explore areas away from the beaten path. So, while these are both reasonable precautions against helpless isolation, they limit one's freedom to explore or find privacy.

A good sailor tries to avoid running onto a shoal but also carries enough gear to get under way should he be grounded. The experienced off-roader learns that, in addition to caution, he also needs tools, supplies, and some basic mechanical skills.

I have assisted scores of stranded motorists, some on goat trails that no one in his or her right mind would try to traverse alone. Most were new to off-roading, rarely prepared for situations they would encounter, and often surprised that their vehicle would "dare fail in such a place." Their initial looks of relief at being "found" quickly changed to concern for the vehicle and the prospect of abandoning it where it could be stripped or stolen.

A vehicle that is not seriously damaged can usually be made to run. I have often wondered, as a stranded motorist drove off amazed and grateful, if the owner of the vehicle ever left pavement again and if he learned from the experience. I hoped he would continue to enjoy the outdoors, but with more caution, better preparedness, and improved mechanical skill.

This book has been written for individuals who travel sparsely populated regions of the country and want to avoid life-threatening situations, unnecessary expense, or disruption of travel caused by mechanical failure. I hope every reader gains useful information to make his or her travel safer and more enjoyable.

RESPONSIBILITY OF OWNER

As the owner and driver of an off-road vehicle (ORV), you are responsible for the safety and actions of your passengers.

Your passengers will assume you have properly maintained the vehicle, will not subject them to danger, and can return them safely home. Passengers may contribute a few bucks for beer, food, or gas, but almost always leave responsibility for general safety to the owner of the vehicle. To this extent you, like the captain of a ship, have a legal obligation to take "reasonable precaution" against causing injury to passengers or damage to the environment.

PLANNING
Before you leave for remote areas, make sure someone knows your planned route and time of return. This person should be instructed to call the Forest Service or appropriate authorities if you do not return by an agreed time.

You should thoroughly research and plan your route by reviewing U.S. Forest Service or U.S. Geological Survey topographic maps. Always stop at a Forest Service office before entering an unfamiliar area. The stop will be worth it. It is always better to learn of rock slides, locked gates, and special regulations before you waste most of a day or get fined. Most offices have free maps of authorized ORV trails. Rangers will review trails with you and often volunteer information about everything from local fishing tips to sites of interest you are likely to miss without their coaching.

You should have enough foresight to carry tools, equipment, and supplies as protection against injury and loss of life.

MECHANICAL KNOWLEDGE
You should be familiar with the design of your vehicle. You should know where important parts of your vehicle are located and how to complete basic repairs. This information can be found in any of the aftermarket manuals published for your specific make and model of vehicle. John Muir Publications, Inc. publishes good, easy-to-understand repair manuals for Toyota pickups (including four-wheel-drive models) and Subaru.

If you are without mechanical skill, you should not venture into remote areas alone. Travel with at least one other vehicle or stay on commonly used trails.

MECHANICAL CONDITION OF VEHICLE
Even if you regularly service your vehicle, check it over thoroughly before you leave the comfort of civilization. It is a lot easier to top off fluids, inspect hoses, and repair wire connections at home.

The temporary repairs suggested in this book will allow you to drive your vehicle but may reduce its level of performance. Before you attempt to "limp" along with poorly running equipment, evaluate the route you plan to take. Do not compound your problem by tackling dangerous terrain that can result in an accident or injury. The final chapter of this book contains a true story about narrowly escaping death when attempting to drive without brakes.

THE ENVIRONMENT

You are also responsible for the actions of everyone in your party. If your passengers cause a fire, throw trash, or chop down vegetation, you can be fined. Most states will even seize your vehicle for hunting and fishing violations committed by a passenger.

Follow the rules, stay on authorized trails, and leave the area the way you found it. You have a moral responsibility to preserve our wilderness for future generations.

How to Use this Manual

As you review the table of contents, you will notice this manual covers two general topics. Part I contains instruction for the diagnosis and repair of mechanical failures that could leave you stranded. Part II provides information to help you improve your wilderness skills.

WILDERNESS SKILLS

Part II presents first aid, survival, and conservation information that is pertinent to off-roading. Each of these topics is big enough to fill its own book, and this manual is by no means all inclusive. The information in this manual is a good start, but I encourage you to investigate other sources as well. The more knowledge you gain about the wilderness, the more you will be at home away from civilization. An improved sense of security can only help you enjoy the outdoors even more.

There have been a number of good books published by the Red Cross, military, conservation groups, and others that will augment your knowledge.

In some areas doctors associated with the Red Cross conduct special first-aid classes for outdoorsmen. One held in southern California is designed for yachtsmen cruising around the world and covers everything from emergency appendectomies to childbirth. If you pass an in-depth first-aid course, some physicians will provide you with prescription emergency medications for use during extended stays in the wilderness.

Learning outdoor skills is a lifelong undertaking. No matter how much you read, you have to apply the knowledge to become truly skillful, and this takes time in the out-of-doors.

If you do not like to read or take classes, you should at least "shoot the bull" with every old-timer you find in the wilderness. Old-timers often possess a wealth of knowledge and welcome the opportunity to share it with someone.

REPAIRS

Before you do anything else, fill in the technical information on the following chart. This step will ensure that you have important repair data with you when consulting the manual. Read the appropriate chapter(s) thoroughly before you begin a course of action. If you study the problem first, you will increase your chances of a successful field repair.

Most people are intimidated by all the "hoses and stuff" crammed under the hood of newer vehicles. Most of what you see upon first opening the hood is part of the emission system and will rarely prevent your vehicle from running. The task of making repairs will be greatly simplified if you concentrate only on those basic parts or systems

Tuneup Specifications	Vehicle 1	Vehicle 2
Timing:		
Spark Plug Gap:		
Point/Reluctor Gap:		
Firing Order:		

Capacities

Oil Pan:		
Transmission:		
Radiator:		

Notes:

_____

_____

_____

that can prevent your vehicle from being driven back to civilization.

With the introduction of oscilloscopes, meters, and computerized diagnostics, most new mechanics no longer learn how to troubleshoot automotive failures without instruments. These skills are becoming an arcane science possessed by only a few "backyard" mechanics who cannot justify the cost of sophisticated equipment.

The repair methods employed in this manual have been used by professional mechanics for more than a half century and still work today. These techniques are ideal for making emergency repairs under primitive trailside conditions. With only a fundamental understanding of automotive systems, the right tools, a little logic, and tips included in this manual, most mechanical failures can be temporarily repaired.

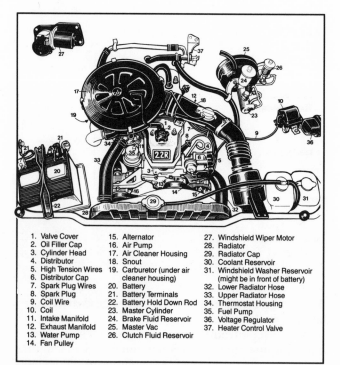

1. Valve Cover	15. Alternator	27. Windshield Wiper Motor
2. Oil Filler Cap	16. Air Pump	28. Radiator
3. Cylinder Head	17. Air Cleaner Housing	29. Radiator Cap
4. Distributor	18. Snout	30. Coolant Reservoir
5. High Tension Wires	19. Carburetor (under air	31. Windshield Washer Reservoir
6. Distributor Cap	cleaner housing)	(might be in front of battery)
7. Spark Plug Wires	20. Battery	32. Lower Radiator Hose
8. Spark Plug	21. Battery Terminals	33. Upper Radiator Hose
9. Coil Wire	22. Battery Hold Down Rod	34. Thermostat Housing
10. Coil	23. Master Cylinder	35. Fuel Pump
11. Intake Manifold	24. Brake Fluid Reservoir	36. Voltage Regulator
12. Exhaust Manifold	25. Master Vac	37. Heater Control Valve
13. Water Pump	26. Clutch Fluid Reservoir	
14. Fan Pulley		

TYPICAL ENGINE COMPARTMENT

All diagrams, illustrations, and tests are based on common system designs. If you do not recognize parts in the illustrations or your vehicle is designed differently, use your service manual as another reference. Basic principles of automotive engineering are universal, and suggested tests or repairs should apply even if your vehicle is slightly different.

Most people have their greatest frustration trying to find the source of a problem. Once they have determined what part has failed, they can often correct it without assistance. Automotive troubleshooting is like most things: the more practice you get, the easier it is. Sidebars in the text are case studies that may let you benefit from my experiences and hopefully will save you some frustration.

You may be surprised how easy it is to apply "process of elimination" logic to the problem. Every automotive system can be proved to work or not. If you concentrate on proving your suspicions before you act, you will save time and nerves and learn a lot about emergency automotive repairs. There are a few simple rules to follow:

- Be patient and thorough.
- If you suspect it, then test it.
- Do not jump to conclusions.
- Confirm everything.

TOOLS, SUPPLIES, EQUIPMENT

Proper outfitting is an important aspect of planning off-road travel. A 25-cent part can make the difference between a spoiled weekend or continuing on your way. With extremely bad luck, lack of emergency supplies could cost someone's life.

You should always carry the following medical

and highway safety gear, even if you are not going off road:

Emergency Road Gear
- Large first-aid kit
- At least one blanket
- Road flares
- Reflective road markers
- Flashlight/spotlight
- Jumper cables
- Extra fuses and light bulbs

You can never have too many tools with you when you break down. I overhauled my first engine with what is on the following list plus a torque wrench and cylinder hone, so I know these tools will handle most calamities. The continuity tester, 6-foot test leads, and starter switch are useful for repair of many common electrical problems.

Tools
- Pliers with wire cutter
- 6-inch Crescent wrench
- Screwdrivers (regular and Phillips)
- Needle-nose pliers
- Small piece of emery paper
- Locking pliers
- Small socket set with ratchet, extension, and spark-plug socket to fit your vehicle
- Set of combination wrenches
- Distributor wrench (if special tool is needed)
- Continuity tester
- 6-foot lengths of 10-gauge wire with alligator clips at each end
- Pushbutton starter switch

Do not be intimidated by the length of the following list. Your vehicle may already carry some of

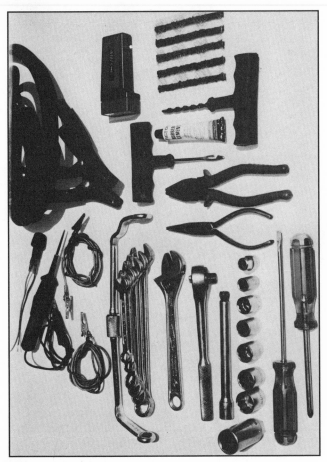

TOOLS

the bulkier items. The rest easily fit in a small tool box or milk crate and can be stored in the garage when you do not need them for off-road travel.

I store the larger items in the vacant space within the engine compartment. Oil, jumper cables, and spare hoses can often be crammed in areas around the wheel wells or radiator.

MISCELLANEOUS SUPPLIES

Miscellaneous Supplies
- Can of starting fluid
- Replacement fan belts
- Two 1-quart cans of motor oil
- Two 1-quart cans of automatic transmission fluid (ATF)
- Can of tire inflator/sealer
- Can of brake fluid
- Duct tape

- Hose clamps (various sizes)
- 3-foot piece of fuel line
- Can of radiator sealant solution
- Tube(s) of "5-minute" epoxy glue
- Strips of epoxy putty
- Spare spark plugs
- Spare ignition points and condenser (or trigger and control module on electronic ignitions)
- Spare ignition coil
- Tire repair kit (plug type)

If your vehicle does not have an automatic transmission, carry two more quarts of motor oil instead of the ATF. Most vehicles require four quarts of lubricant to fill the oil pan.

Experienced off-roaders agree that you must have proper ground tackle to get unstuck. Everyone chooses slightly different off-road equipment to best fit local soil, weather conditions, and terrain.

Before you eliminate any of the items on the following list, I suggest you review my reasons for including them. They may be suitable for your area or provide an extra measure of safety.

Off-Road Equipment
- Chain, rope, or cable— 50 feet or more
- Winch or "come along"
- Two 1-foot x 6-foot pieces Astro Turf or carpet
- Shovel
- 4-foot steel stake or metal fence post
- High lift mechanical jack
- Chains for snow and mud

The survival gear I carry is even longer than the list below and includes a small day backpack and items to make a hike more comfortable. You will probably also add a few items to make your activities

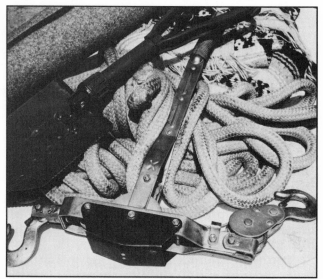

OFF-ROAD GEAR

more enjoyable. A friend of mine never goes anywhere without aspirins, antacid tablets, and mole-
skin.

The important items on the list are food, water,
clothing, and blankets. If you have someone who
will report you overdue, these provisions should
guarantee your survival until rescued. Other
"comfort" or "luxury" items will help if you have to
go for help or survive for extended periods without
the vehicle.

> Survival Gear
> • Good USGA topographic map of area
> • Sleeping bag(s) or blankets
> • Compass
> • Bic-type cigarette lighter
> • Salt tablets
> • Water purification tablets
> • Venom extractor pump

- Heavy blade knife
- 8-foot x 10-foot clear plastic sheet
- Garbage bags— bright color
- Walking shoes on all passengers
- Warm clothing for all passengers
- 5 gallons of extra gas
- 5 gallons of water
- High-calorie food

SPARE PARTS

Talk to people with the same make and model vehicle, but more miles, about mechanical problems they have had. Someone else's mechanical failures will provide insight into the problems you are likely to experience. Parts on similar makes and models often wear out at roughly the same mileage. With this intelligence you can assess the odds of developing specific mechanical problems.

Evaluate the difficulty of replacing the parts that you believe may fail by consulting your repair manual. If you think it is possible to replace the part with tools you carry and you have the room, you might as well include the parts in your list of repair gear.

You can buy parts at an automotive parts store for less than a mechanic would charge if he supplied them. And if you supply your mechanic with the part, labor costs are often lower.

Manufacturers often use the same parts on several models and only change their design with the introduction of a new engine. If you trade your vehicle for a newer one of the same make, the spare parts from your old vehicle are likely to fit.

If you prefer not to spend money on new parts that may get "beaten up" off-road, you can carry used parts with you. Most people never ask their mechanics for the old parts after a tune-up. The old parts make perfect spares; and although they may be in marginal condition, they will get you home.

It is your decision how much to carry. If your vehicle is approaching 50,000 miles, and you intend to use it off road, you should probably carry at least some of the more common parts that unexpectedly fail.

Spare Parts Checklist
- Distributor cap and rotor
- Starter relay
- Starter solenoid
- Radiator hoses
- Voltage regulator
- Water pump

_____

_____

_____

PART 1

DIAGNOSIS
AND
REPAIR

1

Engine Turns Over
But Fails to Start

If the engine cranks but fails to start, the first thing to do is conserve battery current. Be patient. Battery current is one of your most valuable resources and cannot be replenished unless someone is around to give you a jump start.

When stalled on a steep hill, it may be safest to stay where you are until you get the engine running. Your power brakes and steering will not be functional, and moving the vehicle may be dangerous.

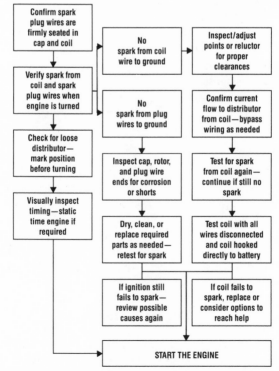

DIAGNOSE AND CORRECT IGNITION FAILURE CHART

Probable Causes	Symptoms	No Sound if Key Turn	Click When Key Turn	No Accessories Worl	Starter Chatters	Starter Spins Free	Starter Grinds
Totally Discharged Battery		X		X			
Low Battery			X		X	X	
Corroded Battery Terminals		X	X	X	X	X	
Loose Ammeter Leads		X		X			
Blown Fuse(s)		X		X			
Bad Starter Relay			X				
Faulty or Sticky Solenoid			X		X		
Sticky or Worn Starter Drive						X	X
Worn Ring Gear						X	X
Burned Out Starter			X				
Loose Starter Wires		X	X				

SYMPTOM CHART

Always put the vehicle in Neutral or Park with the emergency brake engaged before beginning repairs.

Symptoms exhibited just before the trouble started may help to locate the problem. If your starter turns the engine, then the problem must be located in either the fuel system or the ignition system.

Test the ignition system using the methods described in this chapter. The above diagnostic charts will help you locate the cause of the problem.

TESTING IGNITION

Check to ensure the spark plug wires are firmly seated in the distributor cap and coil. Feel the ignition coil to see if it is hot to the touch. On General

Motors (GM) V-8 vehicles made after 1976 with high energy ignitions (HEI), the coil is integrated into the top of the distributor cap. If the coil seems hotter than other items in the same area, it may be shorting out internally. We will test the coil later in this section.

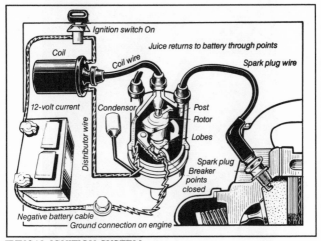

Ignition switch On

Juice returns to battery through points

Coil

Coil wire

Spark plug wire

12-volt current

Condensor

Post

Rotor

Lobes

Distributor wire

Spark plug
Breaker
points
closed

Negative battery cable

Ground connection on engine

TYPICAL IGNITION SYSTEM

Remove the coil wire (spark plug wire on GM HEI distributors) from the distributor cap and slide the rubber end cover back to expose the metal at the end of the wire. Hold the coil wire about 1/4 inch from a ground but not touching it. Turn the engine over with the starter.

Yes, you can get an electrical shock from the spark plug wires and output from the ignition coil. If you are careful not to ground the wire through your body, you should not get zapped. Wear shoes and hold the wire's insulation with a dry rag, gloves, or insulated pliers to prevent getting "tickled."

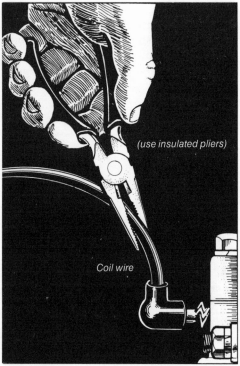

(use insulated pliers)

Coil wire

COIL TEST

To my knowledge, shock from an ignition system has never caused injury to healthy individuals. I once knew a mechanic who would stop running farm implements by grounding out the spark plugs with his arm. I do not recommend you try this to test your machismo, but it should make you a little more comfortable when conducting this test.

There should be a good strong spark across the gap you created from the end of the wire to a ground. The spark should easily jump 1/2-inch and should be a bright white color in daylight or cobalt blue in the dark. A yellowish, weak spark may not create enough heat to ignite fuel in the engine.

If you do not get a good spark from the coil wire, you know there is something faulty with the coil and/or points and condenser (or trigger module). Go to "No Spark from Coil Wire," below.

Replace the coil wire and try the same thing with several spark plug wires.

If there is a strong spark from the coil wire, but not from the spark plug leads, you know the coil and points (or trigger module) are working properly but the rotor and cap are not directing current to the spark plugs. Go to "No Spark from Plug Wires," below.

If you are getting a good spark at the spark plugs, there is probably nothing wrong with your ignition system. Odds are the problem is located in the fuel system, but you should also check the distributor just to confirm that it is not loose and the timing has not slipped.

With a screwdriver, make a scratch at the distributor base to mark the location of the distributor. Give the distributor base a firm twist to see if it is loose. If the distributor does not turn, replace the spark plug wires and continue with "Fuel System," below.

If the distributor is loose, the ignition timing may have moved enough to prevent the engine from starting. If the performance of the engine gradually deteriorated until it stopped, this may be the explanation. Move the distributor back to its original marked location and go to "Static Ignition Timing," below.

No Spark from Plug Wires

If you have confirmed that the ignition is producing spark from the coil but it is not going through the spark plug wires, then a short or poor connection is blocking current flow through the distributor cap.

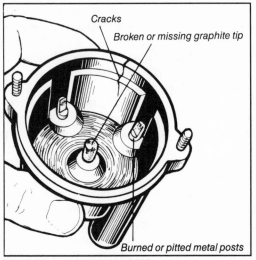

Cracks

Broken or missing graphite tip

Burned or pitted metal posts

INSPECT CAP FOR MALADIES

Remove the distributor cap and look for any of the following problems:

1. Corroded wire ends can weaken or stop current flow. Clean the ends of the wires, one at a time, being careful not to mix them up. Sometimes old wires short out through the insulation and work temporarily if "loomed" away from nearby grounds or wires.

When I was 16 and bought my first car, I discovered the importance of good spark plug wires.

I replaced the points, condenser, cap, and spark plugs to make it run better. When the tune-up was completed, it had a high revolution-per-minute (RPM) misfire and would not idle smoothly. I was convinced that I had connected the spark plug wires wrong or done something to make it run so badly.

I worked into the night trying to find the problem. Then in the darkness, with the engine idling, I witnessed a miniature fireworks display in dozens of places around the engine.

The silicone/graphite core wires had baked hard with age. When I bent them to change the spark plugs and cap, the graphite cores cracked in dozens of places. With increased resistance from all the breaks, current shorted through the old wire insulation to any nearby ground. Because of this experience, I now install only solid metal wires on the engines of my vehicles.

An off-road vehicle will develop the same problem from constant jarring over rough terrain, especially if it is fitted with old and brittle graphite wires.

2. Condensation under the cap will prevent most ignitions from working properly. If the vehicle has been parked in humid weather this is often the problem. Dry the area and reinstall the cap.

3. Carbon fouling can conduct electricity so the rotor and cap misdirect current flow. This problem usually is noticeable as random engine sputtering or misfiring. Most of the carbon probably came from the graphite contact in the top of the cap.

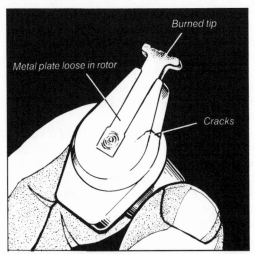

ROTOR MALADIES

Inspect the graphite contact in the cap to confirm that it is connecting with the rotor. If it appears worn out, install a new cap. If you do not have a new cap, clean away the carbon and try to start the vehicle.

4. Cracks or breaks in the rotor or cap can cause the ignition to short out internally. While the crack may have been there for some time, it often does not cause a problem until the vehicle is parked for a while or the humidity is high.

Barely visible hairline cracks will absorb moisture, allowing ignition coil current to ground through the base of the distributor. A good cleaning and airing in the sun will often dry a bad cap and make it function. Replace the rotor and cap if you have a spare set.

When you have a strong spark at the plug wires, start the engine.

A car I once owned developed strange problems every time it rained or the humidity was high. I had just replaced the distributor cap and rotor as part of a complete tune-up and was completely baffled by a lack of spark at the plug wires. I tried everything to get the ignition to work. The points, coil, and wiring all checked out.

Finally, out of frustration I removed the distributor and held it in my hand with all the wires connected and the ignition switch turned on.

When I turned the distributor drive gear, I caught the full coil charge.

Upon closer inspection I discovered a barely detectable manufacturing flaw in the rotor where it slips over the distributor shaft. Moisture would collect under the metal contact of the rotor, shorting to the distributor shaft rather than directing current to the spark plug wires.

Your ORV can develop the same problem,

especially if it has been parked overnight in humid weather.

No Spark from Coil Wire

With the distributor cap removed, engage the starter for a short while and observe the mechanical operation of the distributor.

Dirty or burned ignition points will cause intermittent failure of the ignition. Even a small amount of oil can prevent proper contact at the points. Clean the point contacts with a dry, clean piece of paper. If they are extremely pitted and burned, file them with an ignition file or emery cloth. Replace badly burned points if you carry a spare set. If you do not have a feeler gauge, you can use a piece of paper from this book as a makeshift gauge.

Makeshift Gauge
Single Thickness   = .005 in./.137 mm
Double Thickness   = .011 in./.273 mm
Triple Thickness   = .016 in./.410 mm

Points that do not open or close correctly will make it impossible for the engine to fire. If the points do not open, usually due to wear, you will have to adjust them. A piece of paper from this book can be used as a makeshift gauge.

A distributor shaft that does not turn indicates a stripped distributor drive inside the engine. Inspect the distributor base to make sure it is firmly seated in the engine block. This could also cause the ignition timing to change. Loose distributors have been known to rise straight up, thereby disengaging from the distributor drive. If the distributor has disengaged in this manner, it will need to be retimed. See "Static Ignition Timing," below.

If the distributor is firmly seated but the shaft does not turn when the engine turns over, correction

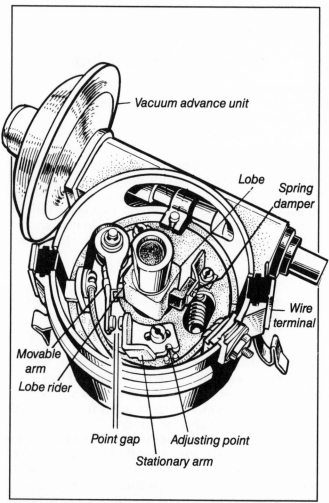

Vacuum advance unit

Lobe

Spring damper

Wire terminal

Movable arm

Lobe rider

Point gap   Adjusting point

Stationary arm

CONTACT POINT DISTRIBUTOR

will require removal of the distributor and replacement of the lower drive. It is doubtful you will be able to correct this problem on the roadside.

Correct any of the above conditions and check

again for coil spark. If the coil still will not spark, continue with the appropriate following section, "Ignition Points Distributor Repair" or "Breakerless Ignition Repair."

Breakerless Ignition Repair

If your engine has breakerless electronic ignition and the coil will not spark, inspect the system in

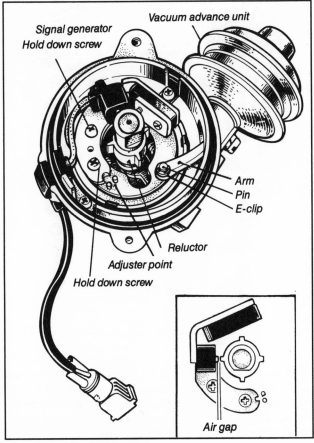

BREAKERLESS DISTRIBUTOR

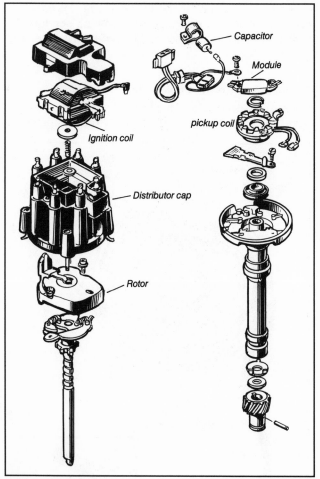

Capacitor

Module

pickup coil

Ignition coil

Distributor cap

Rotor

HEI DISTRIBUTOR

and around the distributor for loose wires or misadjusted tolerances. Breakerless ignitions are far more reliable than point ignitions, but it is not possible to repair their solid-state components. If a component fails, it must be replaced. I therefore recommend that you carry spare distributor parts for your electronic ignition in the event the pickup unit, control module, or HEI coil fails. A complete set of replacement components for most American cars requires a total investment of only $40— a worthwhile investment compared to the expense of towing.

Confirm Current to Coil

Always confirm electrical current to the distributor. With the ignition switch turned to "on," use your continuity tester to confirm there is power to the hot (+) terminal on the coil. Connect the clip of the tester to any convenient ground. Anything bolted directly to the engine block should make a good ground. Touch the (+) coil terminal with the continuity tester. Not all coils are clearly marked. It is the correct terminal if the wire attached to the other coil terminal (-) goes directly into the base of the distributor. Quickly turn the ignition switch to "start" and back to "on" to confirm that current flow to the coil is not interrupted when the vehicle is being started. If the continuity tester does not light in both the "on" and "start" positions then bypass the ignition switch by connecting a length of wire to the hot (+) side of the battery and the small coil terminal marked (+).

With the bypass wire attached, check again for current at the terminal. If you cannot get the tester to light with the bypass wire connected, there could be a short somewhere that is preventing your tester from lighting. Remove the original wires from the (+) coil terminal and try the spark test again with only the bypass lead connected to the positive (+) coil terminal.

If this was the problem and there is a good spark, you can use your wire bypass as the ignition switch until permanent repairs are made.

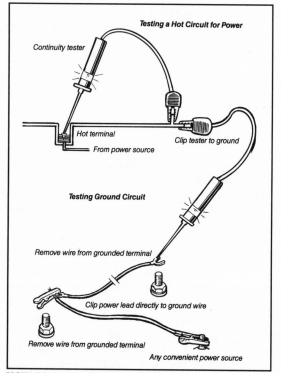

HOW TO USE A CONTINUITY TESTER

Failed Components

If the positive (+) terminal on the coil is getting current but you cannot get a spark from the coil and you have already checked the cap and rotor as instructed earlier, then an electronic component in the system may have failed.

On GM HEI ignitions, remove the coil and confirm that it can make good contact at its base into the distributor cap. This area is prone to corrosion and should be cleaned if dirty.

Some ignition systems, such as that provided on many Chrysler products, have "air gap" adjustments on the trigger unit that must be correctly set to function properly. When you have confirmed proper connections to the components of your electronic ignition, consult your aftermarket service manual for tolerances and adjustments.

If once you have confirmed that there is power to an electronic ignition, that all contacts are clean and gaps properly adjusted, but the vehicle will still not start, there is little left to do at roadside other than begin installing new components. The parts are more prone to failure and should be the first components replaced.

Most electronic ignitions require a full 12 volts to function properly. If you suspect your battery is low, let the vehicle sit for half an hour. A good battery will recharge itself slightly. If the engine turns over slowly but does not start, try attaching a wire lead directly between the positive side of the battery and the positive terminal on the ignition coil to bypass in-line resistance. Hold the choke butterfly open, squirt starting fluid down the carburetor throat and try it again. The additional unrestricted battery current and volatile fuel may be enough to get it started.

IGNITION POINTS DISTRIBUTOR REPAIR

If you cannot get the coil to spark, use the following test method to conserve the charge of your battery.

Test Primary Circuits

Remove the distributor cap and rotor with all the spark plug wires attached. The distributor cap of your vehicle will be held in place by either spring clips that can be pried away from the cap base or springloaded fasteners that must be pushed down with a screwdriver and turned 180 degrees.

Turn the engine until the points are closed. Remove the coil wire from the distributor cap and

slide the rubber end cover back to expose the metal
at the end of the wire. Lay the coil wire about 1/8
inch from a convenient ground on the engine but
not touching it. With the ignition key turned to On,
use your screwdriver to open and close the points
manually, being careful not to make contact across
the points with the screwdriver. This simulates
turning the engine over with the starter but con-
serves valuable battery current. There should be a
detectable spark and "crack" sound from the coil
wire as the points break contact.

Confirm Current to the Coil
If opening and closing the points does not make the
coil fire, then there is a short or a poor wire connection somewhere. The problem could be caused by
the ignition switch, a bad condenser or resistor, or
even a break in wiring.

    With the ignition switch turned to On, use your
continuity tester to confirm power to the hot (+)
terminal on the coil. Connect the clip of the tester
to any convenient ground and touch the (+) terminal. Not all coils are clearly marked. It is the correct
terminal if the wire attached to the other coil terminal (-) goes directly into the base of the distributor.
Quickly turn the ignition switch to "start" and back
to "on" to confirm that you do not lose current flow
to the coil when the vehicle is started.

    If the light does not indicate current flow to the
coil in both the On and Start positions, bypass the
ignition switch by connecting a length of wire to the
hot (+) side of the battery and the positive coil terminal (+). With the bypass wire attached, check
again for current at the terminal. If you cannot get
the tester to light with the bypass connected,
remove the original wires from the terminal. A serious short in the wiring can draw off all power and
prevent your tester from lighting.

Try to get the coil to fire again. If power to the coil was interrupted and now there is a good spark from the coil, you can use your wire bypass as the ignition switch until permanent repairs are made. Refit the distributor cap, rotor, and coil wire and start the vehicle.

Check the Points

Turn the ignition switch to Off. Disconnect the negative (-) wire from the coil. Insert a piece of dry cardboard between the point contacts to hold them open. Connect a test lead between the positive battery terminal and the wire that was on the negative (-) terminal of the coil. This will supply confirmed power to the ignition points. If the test lead sparks when you touch it to the battery terminal or gets hot, there may be a short in the negative coil wire or the points, and you should disconnect the lead immediately.

Your points have current flowing properly if the tester lights when touched to the movable point contact. If the tester does not light, then the points are shorting to the base of the distributor, or the negative wire from the coil is broken. Remove the hot wire from the points and check it for current flow. If the tester lights, you know the short must be located within the point set itself.

Install new points or attempt repair using the following method.

Inspect the insulation around the ignition points, paying close attention to the screw terminal and the pivot peg to insure that they are not grounding. The small fiber "tube" around the pivot pin has been known to wear on the underside, allowing the points to short out. On most ignition point sets it is "press fit" and can be pushed down slightly to keep the moving part of the points from making contact on the base.

If you have confirmed current to the movable

part of the points, remove the cardboard and try to get coil spark. If the coil sparks, reassemble the distributor and start the engine.

Condenser Failure

If the coil will not spark, try it again without the condenser wire connected to the point terminal.

If the coil will spark now, but not when the condenser wire is connected, your condenser is probably faulty. Bad condensers short out internally through their metal case and prevent current from crossing the points.

Disconnect the condenser wire and move it out of the way of rotating parts in the distributor. Refit the cap, rotor, and wire and start the vehicle.

The vehicle will run without the condenser, but eventually the point contacts will burn and become nonfunctional. If the points burn before you reach a location where permanent repairs can be made, file or sand the point contacts so they will pass current again. Be sure to replace the condenser as soon as possible.

Faulty condensers can produce unusual symptoms. They may not always simply stop the engine. One time while I was driving my GMC, it developed an occasional backfire and high speed stall. It always started and revved as normal, but when driven at 60 miles per hour (mph) it would sputter and then backfire as if the key were being turned off.

The engine started easily and idled normally. I was certain there was a loose wire in the ignition that vibrated loose at high speeds to create the symptoms, but everything checked out.

Finally, I changed the condenser, and, sure enough, the problem went away. The condenser only failed from heat generated at higher RPMs. When the engine shut down and RPMs dropped, the condenser quickly cooled and stopped shorting, allowing the engine to run again. If your vehicle develops similar symptoms while being driven off road and you can find nothing wrong with the ignition wiring, then your vehicle may have a bad condenser.

TESTING IGNITION COIL

If you have confirmed current to the coil and from the coil to the distributor, but the coil still will not fire, the coil may be faulty. This is even more probable if upon your first inspection of the ignition system the coil seemed hot to the touch. Bad coils are not common and should be one of the last causes for which to look.

If other more probable causes of the failure have been eliminated, you can use the following test to confirm condition of the coil:

With the ignition turned off, remove the wires from the terminals on the coil. Remove the coil wire from the distributor cap. Lay the wire near, but not touching, a convenient ground. Wire the positive (+) terminal on the coil directly to the battery. Use another wire connected to the negative (-) side of the coil to simulate opening and closing points. Quickly touch, and then remove, the wire from any convenient ground.

If you have a good ground on the spark plug, it should spark each time you remove the wire from ground. If you cannot make the coil spark, it is probably bad and needs to be replaced.

Coils are notorious for intermittent failure and often will work again in a short while when they have cooled off.

My first bad coil experience was with a two-year-old car in rural Wisconsin during the winter.

The car failed in minus 20° F weather on three occasions. Each time it was towed to a garage where the mechanic would push it into a heated service bay and let the snow melt off before he would go to work.

*When it warmed to room temperature, it would start
right up and check out fine on the scope. He insisted it must be vapor lock, but gasoline additive
did not help. I was getting tired of walking to the
nearest telephone for a tow.*

*Finally, after some protesting on my part, the
mechanic put on a new coil and that finally corrected the problem.*

*In cold-weather off-road conditions,a bad coil may
not be hot to the touch and may function again
when warmed up slightly.*

If you carry a spare coil, no problem. Install a
replacement, and off you should go.

STATIC IGNITION TIMING

If the distributor is loose and you suspect it may
have moved, you can do a rough check of the
timing without a timing light.

Turn the engine to the appropriate timing mark
indicated in your repair manual or on the emission
specifications sticker in the engine compartment
(e.g., 10° BTDC). This notation means 10 degrees
before the number one piston is top dead center on
the compression stroke.

Mark on the side of the distributor base where
the number one cylinder wire enters the distributor cap. Remove the distributor cap. Note the location of the rotor. The rotor should be aligned
between the mark you made by the number one
cylinder wire and a point directly opposite. Do
not be concerned if the contact of the rotor
points directly away from the number one cylinder
wire location. This simply means the engine is on
the top of the exhaust stroke, not the compression
stroke. To correct this, simply turn the engine
another complete revolution until the timing marks

are again aligned. The rotor contact should then point toward the number one cylinder wire.

Timing that is advanced too far will make the

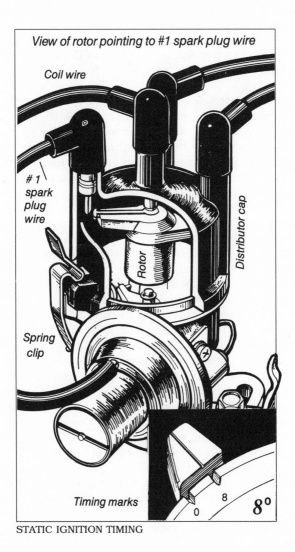

STATIC IGNITION TIMING

engine turn over slowly, almost as if the battery were low. If your engine turns over slowly when starting and you know the battery is fully charged, then you have another reason to suspect the timing has moved.

If it is obvious the timing has changed and you have marked the original location of the distributor as instructed earlier, you can safely attempt to reset the timing.

Turn the engine to the appropriate timing marks (10 degrees BTDC, etc.). Replace the distributor cap and rotor. Remove the number one cylinder spark plug and wire. Lay the spark plug with wire attached on the engine so the spark plug has a good ground connection. Loosen the distributor so it turns easily.

Turn the ignition switch to On and slowly rotate the distributor back and forth past the point where the spark plug fires.

Turn the distributor in the direction the rotor turns during normal operation and then carefully back in the opposite direction until the spark plug fires (simulating normal operation). Note the location of the distributor when the number one spark plug fired. This is roughly where the distributor should be located if the timing is properly set.

Static timing is not as accurate as a timing light, and the specifications in your service manual are based on a running engine with the mechanical advance of the distributor functioning. If the statically timed position is near the mark you made earlier, the original setting was probably correct.

If you are satisfied the timing is now closer to the correct location, replace the spark plug and try to start the engine. **Do not adjust the idle screw.**

When the engine has started and warmed to normal operating temperature, fine-tune the timing by turning the distributor until the idle speed is normal.

If the engine has cooled, make sure the fast idle cam (on carburetors) or cold-start circuits (on injected systems) are in normal operating mode before you make the final adjustment and tighten the distributor.

FUEL SYSTEM

If your vehicle was tuned and running correctly before you went off road, any failure of the fuel

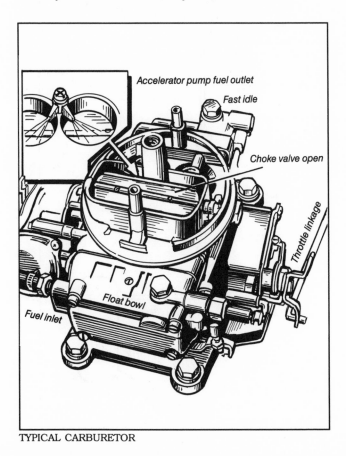

TYPICAL CARBURETOR

system is probably caused by one of the problems listed at the beginning of this chapter.

Most vehicles that are used off road are equipped with carburetors. There are also several fuel-injection systems currently in use. Most

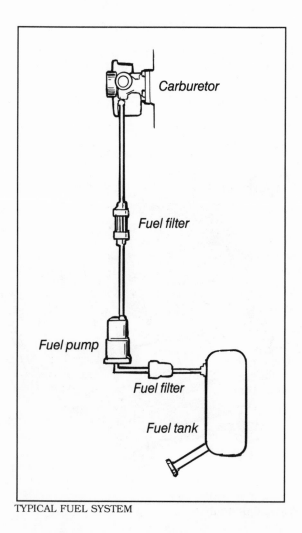

TYPICAL FUEL SYSTEM

injection systems are controlled by solid-state electronics and are impossible to repair if the main control unit fails. Fortunately, a complete failure is rare, and the problems that prevent a fuel-injected vehicle from starting can often be remedied so the vehicle is drivable.

If you have fuel injection, review the troubleshooting section in your service manual, paying closest attention to switches, in-line fuses, and connections that can prevent starting. Many domestic fuel injection systems are equipped with a throttle position switch that can malfunction and in-line fuses that are not located in the main fuse block. If the throttle switch is disconnected or blown fuses are replaced, the vehicle will often start.

ENGINE FLOODING

The problem of engine flooding occurs primarily on carbureted vehicles.

You can confirm flooding is the problem if the engine compartment or tail pipe smells of unburned fuel.

To verify engine flooding, remove one spark plug. If the spark plug is wet, your engine is definitely flooded. If it is dry, skip to "Engine Starved for Fuel."

Fuel-injected vehicles equipped with cold-start injectors can flood because this injector is leaking or does not shut off. If your vehicle is equipped with a cold-start injector, consult your service manual for diagnosis and repair. You can often disconnect electrical current flow or fuel supply to the cold-start injector to prevent continued flooding.

Remove the air cleaner from the top of the carburetor. Check the position of the choke baffle. If the engine is warm, the choke baffle should open. If the choke baffle remains closed when the engine warms up, it will cause the engine to "load up" from excess fuel. Dislodge the choke or disconnect the choke linkage to the baffle so it will open when the engine is warm.

If the choke baffle is in the correct position, use a firm heavy object to tap the carburetor float bowls. This may dislodge the float needles if they are stuck open.

Clearing a Flooded Engine

If the choke butterfly is closed, hold it open while someone depresses the accelerator pedal all the way down and the engine turns over. This serves to provide maximum air flow and will help clear unburned fuel from the cylinders.

Do not pump on the accelerator. Each time you push the accelerator down you will pump more fuel into the engine.

If the battery is low from cranking the engine, remove the spark plugs so the engine will turn over more easily. With spark plugs removed, the engine will also require fewer revolutions to clear.

When the spark plugs have dried, insert them and try to start the engine. If the engine does not start, verify the ignition is firing properly while you wait 15 minutes or longer, and then try the same routine again.

Sticking or Improperly Adjusted Floats

If the engine sputters but will not continue running after it has started, the carburetor floats may still be improperly adjusted or stuck.

A float problem is often more noticeable while driving on a steep grade. If the engine ran roughly when on a grade, you should remove the float assembly from your carburetor and clean it thoroughly. A speck of dirt could have prevented the floats from stopping excess fuel to the engine. If you cannot detect dirt in the float bowls, they may be worn and not sealing properly. This can be verified by turning the float assembly upside down and blowing into the fuel inlet. The weight of the floats should be enough to prevent air from passing the float needles.

Lowering the floats to apply added pressure on the float needles will often serve to keep the vehicle running until the needles can be replaced.

Caution should be used when lowering floats below recommended specifications. While the vehicle may run correctly at low speed, faster highway driving may cause the vehicle to run lean (low fuel-to-air mixture), causing burned valves and engine overheating. Be sure to correct the problem at the earliest possible convenience.

ENGINE STARVED FOR FUEL

If you have confirmed the vehicle is not flooded, check to confirm the engine is getting fuel.

Test for Fuel Flow

If the vehicle is carbureted, there is an easy way to confirm fuel to the engine. Remove the air cleaner and look down the carburetor throat while you move the throttle linkage. On most carburetors an accelerator pump lever extends out the side of the carburetor, and a linkage connected directly to the throttle moves the lever each time you push the accelerator pedal.

You should be able to see fuel squirting into the carburetor each time the throttle is opened. If you cannot see fuel being pumped into the carburetor, the float bowls are dry and the engine is not getting fuel.

Some domestic fuel injection systems inject fuel directly into the intake manifold from a single jet. On these units you should see metered fuel flowing when the engine is being turned over. Check your service manual to

troubleshoot fuel supply to your particular system.

For either fuel-injected or carbureted vehicles, squirt a healthy amount of starting fluid into the carburetor or air intake and try to start the engine. If the engine starts, but only runs a short while, you have confirmed the engine is not getting fuel.

Regaining Fuel Flow

If the engine is hot and you are at a high altitude, your engine may be suffering from vapor lock. When the fuel line gets unusually hot, especially at higher altitudes, the gasoline will vaporize in the line and block fuel flow.

The easiest correction for suspected vapor lock is simply to let the engine cool down. If the problem persists, you can wrap a damp rag around the part of the fuel line you think is getting overheated. The evaporating water often serves to keep the line cool to prevent gasoline vaporization.

If the altitude or temperature is not unusual, you should look for a bad fuel pump or blockage in the line.

Fuel-injected vehicles and some newer carbureted vehicles are equipped with an electric fuel pump that maintains continuous pressure on the system. If your vehicle has an electric fuel pump, confirm that the fuses are OK and the pump is getting current.

Disconnect the main fuel line to the carburetor (or fuel distributor on fuel-injected models). Turn the engine over and watch for fuel being pumped from the line. If the fuel pump is working correctly and lines are not blocked, it should squirt a good-sized stream of fuel.

Vehicles equipped with electric fuel pumps will squirt immediately before the engine turns over if the pump is operating properly.

If fuel squirts readily from the fuel line but the

engine is not getting fuel, then the carburetor fuel
inlet is plugged or there is a malfunction in the fuel-
injection system.

If you have fuel injection, consult the troubleshooting section of the service manual for your
vehicle. Unless you can find an improper circuit
connection, switch, or burned-out fuse, you will
probably not be able to locate or repair the problem
on the trail.

If the vehicle is carbureted, tap on the float
bowls with a heavy object while you blow into the
fuel inlet. You should hear air entering the carburetor. Refit the fuel line and try to start the engine.

If the engine still does not start, you will need to
disassemble the carburetor to determine why the
floats are not allowing fuel flow. Check the service
manual for disassembly instructions. Some older-
model carburetors have covers that allow easy
access to the float bowls.

When you have cleaned and reassembled the
carburetor, start the vehicle. If fuel does not pump
from the line at the carburetor, follow the fuel line
toward the fuel pump and check for plugged filters
or obstructions.

Remove the line on the outlet side of the fuel
pump. If fuel squirts directly from the pump when
the engine is turned over, there is a blockage between the pump and the carburetor.

If you suspect the fuel filter is plugged, you can
temporarily bypass it with a short piece of fuel line
and then check for fuel flow again.

**You should not run unfiltered fuel through
fuel-injected systems. Always make sure there is
at least one filter still in the fuel line on injected
vehicles. Even small particles can permanently
plug injectors.**

If you cannot get fuel from the outlet side of the
fuel pump, remove the inlet line connected to the
pump. Attach one end of a length of hose to the inlet

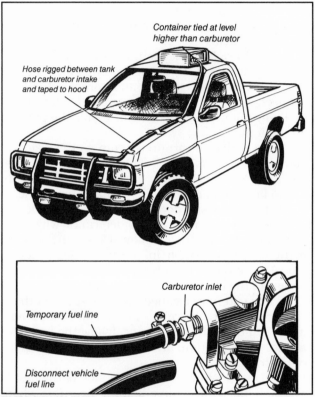

Container tied at level
higher than carburetor

Hose rigged between tank
and carburetor intake
and taped to hood

Carburetor inlet

Temporary fuel line

Disconnect vehicle
fuel line

EMERGENCY FUEL SYSTEM

side of the fuel pump, with the other end immersed
in a container of fuel. If the fuel pump still does not
pump, it has failed and needs to be replaced.

Replace the pump if you have a spare with you.
If the vehicle is fuel injected and you do not have
another fuel pump, consider your options for
getting help. The fuel-injection system will not work
unless it is pressurized. The fuel system on carbureted vehicles, though, does not need to be
pressurized. You can drive away by using a fuel

can or any convenient container as a gravity flow tank connected to the fuel inlet on the carburetor.

Mount the tank or container with wire or duct tape in any convenient location above the carburetor. You now have the original gravity flow fuel system used on early cars. Providing you do not go up hills so steep the tank is below the carburetor, you should make it to a garage.

If you have confirmed that the fuel pump works, connect a piece of hose to the fuel line leading to the tank and blow in the line to verify that there is no blockage between the gas tank and the fuel pump.

When you blow, someone listening at the fuel filler neck should hear bubbling. Blowing in the line may also help dislodge any gunk.

I once bought an exotic sports car that had the gas tank sending unit installed with silicone gasket sealer. Silicone sealer expands to about ten times its original size when soaked in gasoline. The car mysteriously died on several occasions, and it would require this technique of blowing down the fuel line to get it started.

Every time I flushed the tank and was convinced the tank was clean, it would eventually stall again. To find the problem, I completely removed the tank from the car and discovered the cause. Small pellets of silicone sealer from the sending-unit gasket would swell in the fuel, fall off, and then block the fuel pickup.

This same problem can happen off road with older recreational vehicles. Older recreational vehicles are often not used for extended periods and will develop rust scale inside the gas tank. The rust scale can dislodge while bouncing off road and plug the fuel pickup.

If you are satisfied that the fuel line is open from the tank to the pump and from the pump to the carburetor, you should be able to start the vehicle. Be aware that a blockage of the fuel line is likely to happen again until the tank is thoroughly flushed.

2

Engine Does Not Turn Over

When stalled on a steep hill, it may be safest to stay where you are until you get the engine running. Power brakes and steering will not be functional, and moving the vehicle may be dangerous. Always put the vehicle in Neutral or Park with the emergency brake engaged before beginning repairs.

If the area is inhabited by snakes, remember that they will crawl under the vehicle to escape the midday sun. Carefully inspect the ground under the vehicle before you crawl or reach where they may be resting.

Symptoms / Ignition Failures	Exhaust Backfiring	Intake Backfiring	Ignition Misfiring	Engine Pinging	Low Power	Overheating
Failed Condenser	X		X			
Timing Too Retarded	X				X	X
Timing Too Advanced		X		X		
Poor Ignition Point Contact			X		X	
Faulty Module/Reluctor Gap			X			
Bad Spark Plug Wire(s)			X			
Fouled/Cracked Distributor Cap or Rotor			X			
Bad Ignition Coil			X			
Fuel System Failures						
Engine Flooded with Fuel - Flooding Carb Floats - Choke Stuck Closed - Faulty Cold Start Valve			X		X	
Engine Starved for Fuel - Vapor Lock - Fuel Line or Filter Blockage - Bad Fuel Pump (or Fuse)		X	X	X	X	X

SYMPTOM CHART

Use the chart of symptoms and probable causes to help isolate the reason your engine fails to turn over.

TEST THE BATTERY CHARGE

A low battery charge or poor cable connection is the leading cause of the failure of an engine to turn over, so this is the logical place to start.

Try the windshield wipers or headlights to determine whether the battery is providing current to the electrical system. If everything works normally, the battery charge and terminal connections are probably OK.

You can touch the terminals on any 12-volt battery without getting shocked. Unless you are standing in water, with wet hands, you cannot feel the current in a 12-volt battery. The following test is safe and requires no insulation from current flow.

If the wipers seem sluggish or the headlights are dim, check the battery charge and cable connections by **quickly** shorting between the cable ends with a wrench or pliers.

The battery should spark strongly when your wrench touches both posts. If it does not, the battery has lost its charge or the battery connections are corroded and not making a good contact. Check the terminal connections and clean as necessary. Also check the battery cable connections to the starter, starter relay (if so equipped), and engine ground.

Many people forget about the other end of the battery cables. If the battery wires are not firmly bolted to the block or the starter, symptoms will be produced that are similar to a low battery charge or failing parts.

DEAD BATTERY

You will have trouble getting the vehicle started if you have confirmed good battery cable connections but the battery charge is so low that relays and accessories do not work.

Starting your engine will be doubly difficult under these circumstances if it is equipped with an electronic ignition. Most electronic ignitions require a full 12 volts to function properly.

When you know your battery is low from cranking the engine or leaving the lights on, let the vehicle sit for half an hour or more while you study the rest of this chapter. A good battery will re-charge itself slightly and may turn the engine again if allowed to rest.

An engine that barely turns over may start if you hold the choke butterfly open and squirt a small amount of starting fluid down the carburetor intake while someone turns the engine over. The more volatile fuel may help start the engine, but it can also cause flooding, so do not overdo it.

If your vehicle has a manual transmission, try pushstarting it down the nearest slope. A low gear will turn the engine faster on pavement, but on gravel it may simply lock up the rear drive wheels. Use a higher gear when on loose gravel to insure that the engine turns and that you can maintain control of the vehicle down the grade.

If you cannot get the engine to turn over, your options are to abandon your vehicle or wait for help to come.

STARTER CLICKS WHEN KEY IS TURNED

If you have confirmed that the battery is charged and its terminals are clean, but the system only clicks when the key is turned, you should first suspect the starter relay or solenoid.

There are two common starters currently in use. Some designs have the starter relay attached to the starter; others have a separate starter relay located in the engine compartment, usually on a fender well. Most starters are solenoid actuated. When the ignition switch is turned to "start," current is directed to the solenoid plunger which then connects the large battery lead to the motor windings and engages the starter drive gear to the flywheel of the engine.

You can easily tell the design with which your vehicle is equipped by noting the number of wires attached to the starter. If only the large positive battery cable runs to the starter, then your vehicle has a remote starter relay. The relay will always be located somewhere along the positive battery cable between the battery and starter.

Turn the ignition switch to Off and put the vehicle in Park or Neutral. Check to see if the starter works, by using a screwdriver or wrench to make contact between the terminals on the starter or remote-mount starter relay. There will be sparks, and your tool may stick to the terminals. This action bypasses starter circuits that may be malfunctioning but does not interfere with the ignition system. If the engine turns over using this method, you should be able to start the vehicle with the ignition switch turned to On. Other than minor damage to the tool, this starting method is harmless.

If your vehicle has a remote-mount starter relay, you may be able to start the vehicle more conveniently using the following method.

Connect one end of a wire to the positive (+) side of the battery. Touch the small wire terminals on the relay until the relay clicks and the starter turns. The wire bypass can be used to start the engine without melting your tools on the high amperage starter terminals. Be careful to remove the wire when the engine is running so the starter disengages.

No Sound When Key Is Turned

If you have ever tried to start your vehicle and found everything completely dead, you know how the heart skips a beat. There is comfort in even the slightest sign of life. When none of the accessories work, the situation seems much worse. But, unless you have left your lights on or have cranked the battery dead, chances are the problem is minor.

Most vehicles have at least one relay that clicks when the ignition key is inserted and turned. Without this relay to shut off power when you park, accessories and the alternator would drain the battery.

There are few possible causes for complete silence when the key is turned:

- Completely dead battery
- Corroded battery terminal connections
- Blown main fusible link from battery
- Lost of power to ignition switch and main relay

Following directions, you should have already eliminated the first two possibilities and have confirmed that battery current is available.

FUSES

Power to the vehicle is supplied by a small wire directly connected to either the battery or to the starter cable. Most vehicles have a fuse in the power wire near the battery.

The fuse may be held in a plastic holder, or it may be a fusible link molded into a wire. A fusible link is a section of wire designed to melt away at a predetermined current load and to be replaced if it fails.

If necessary, consult the wiring schematic in your service manual to locate the main power supplies coming from the positive terminal on the

battery and all in-line fusible links that may have
blown.

Use the continuity tester to confirm current
past fuses and fusible links. If you find a fuse that
has blown, replace it and try to start the vehicle.

**Bypassing fuses is not recommended. Whatever overloaded the circuit in the first place
could start a fire or burn wires without the fuse
for protection. If you must drive the vehicle
without properly installed fuses, avoid operation of accessories and carefully watch for
smoke or fire.**

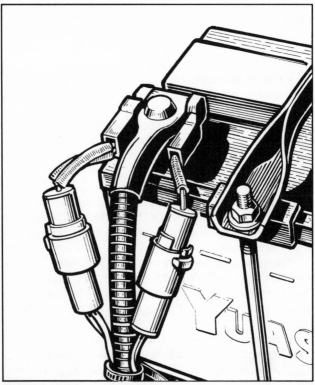

FUSIBLE LINKS

LOSS OF POWER TO IGNITION SWITCH AND MAIN RELAY

If you have confirmed that current will flow through the in-line fusible links, then there should be current at the starter and starter relay, which are fed through the large positive (+) battery cable.

Locate the wire that provides current to the circuits of the vehicle (it should lead from the starter relay or first junction connected to the large positive (+) battery wire).

With the ignition switch and radio turned on, begin hunting for the wiring problem. If you jiggle the right wires, the radio may turn on and off as the circuit is completed and then broken. This technique can serve as a "homing device" to locate the problem. When the radio and other accessories work normally, the vehicle should start.

Follow the power source toward the engine compartment firewall. Check for current with the continuity tester as you go. Check all plug connectors under the dash, especially connections on the back of the ammeter and fuse blocks. You should eventually be able to locate the wiring problem.

If all else fails, and you cannot find the problem, you can bypass all the wiring to get the vehicle started. Connect a lead between the positive (+) battery terminal and the positive (+) coil terminal. Turn the ignition switch to On. Engage the starter using the method(s) discussed above, "Starter Clicks When Key Is Turned." Once the engine starts, all accessories including your lights may work.

This past summer I was with friends in the southern Sierras, just south of Golden Trout Wilderness area. We had traveled several miles through rough terrain in an attempt to reach a meadow with a stream that was reportedly full of 13-inch golden trout. The truck was running fine.

We parked to investigate a steep, narrow spot in

the trail and decided the road was not passable.
When we got into the truck and I turned the key,
nothing happened, not even a click. I tried the horn,

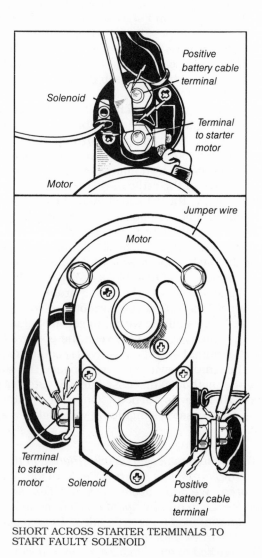

SHORT ACROSS STARTER TERMINALS TO
START FAULTY SOLENOID

radio, and wipers without success. The vehicle was completely dead.

My first reaction was to check the battery and terminal connections. Everything looked normal, but I cleaned the terminals anyway. I checked the fuse panel, and all was normal. Everything was still dead.

I began following the hot lead back from the battery, checking fuses as I went, through the firewall, and under the dash. There was current to the starter and starter relay. When I bypassed the ignition switch, the starter would turn over, but the engine would not start.

As I checked the wire connector plugs under the dash, I noticed the dome light would flicker on and off. I jiggled wires until I found the problem using the light as a "homing" device.

A nut holding the power supply wire to the back of the ammeter had shaken loose on the rough road. When the engine was running the alternator powered everything through other circuits. Once the engine was turned off, there was no current to the ignition switch, or from the ignition switch to the relay that turned everything on.

When the nut was tightened, everything worked as usual and we were back on our way to find the trout.

I could have used a wire lead connected between the battery and the coil to provide ignition, but it would have been inconvenient. If you experience a similar situation where the entire vehicle is dead, but the battery seems charged and there is power through the engine compartment firewall, check the connection at the back of your ammeter. On most vehicles the ignition and accessories will not work if this wire falls off.

STARTER SPINS FREE

There are few reasons for a starter to spin free without engaging to the flywheel. A low current supply or a faulty starter solenoid is usually the cause. You can often locate the problem by the sound the starter makes when it is first turned on.

Some starters spin slowly and do not engage if the power supply is low. The sound of the starter will be low pitched, and you may actually hear it accelerate. To correct this condition, verify that the battery is fully charged and cable connections to the starter are good.

An immediate "snap" to full RPMs indicates the current supply is good, but a faulty solenoid is producing unusual symptoms. To find out how to correct this condition, continue reading the next section.

STARTER CHATTERS OR GRINDS

STARTER CHATTER

Starter chatter can be caused by low power supply or a faulty solenoid. The solenoid plunger makes intermittent contact and cycles back and forth without fully engaging the starter drive gear to the flywheel.

Verify the battery is fully charged and cable connections to the starter are good. If you have confirmed full power to the starter, but the chatter persists, then the solenoid is probably faulty. Most solenoids cannot be taken apart or fixed, but the following may force it to work temporarily.

Turn the ignition switch off and place the vehicle in Park or Neutral. Use a screwdriver or wrench to provide contact between the large and small terminals on the starter. There will be sparks, and your tool may stick to the terminals. This may bypass faulty contacts inside the solenoid and allow the starter to engage. Other than damage to the tool, the method is harmless.

If the engine turns over using this method, you

should be able to start the vehicle with the ignition switch turned to On.

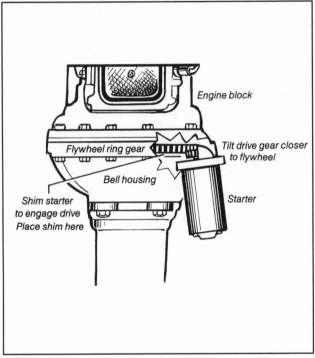

STARTER SHIM

GRINDING NOISES

If the starter spins free or makes grinding noises like gears that do not mesh, it is not fully engaging to the flywheel of the engine. This can be caused by a sticky or worn starter drive gear, or by missing teeth on the flywheel.

To correct these problems you must first remove

the starter. Clean the starter drive with gasoline. While the starter is out, inspect the ring gear to see if teeth are worn off the flywheel where it has stopped.

If flywheel teeth are worn off, place the car in Neutral and, with the parking brake on, use a screwdriver to move the flywheel so good teeth are showing. Most engines turn clockwise, so rotate the damaged teeth toward the side that will provide nearly a complete revolution of the engine before the bad spot comes around again. Inertia will often carry the engine past the bad spot once it starts spinning. Who knows? The engine may even stop in a different place the next time you turn it off. If it does not, you can rotate the engine at the fan or remove the cover on the lower front of the bell housing to gain easier access to the fly-wheel.

Inspect the starter drive gear for wear. If the starter drive-gear teeth or bushings are worn sufficiently so as not to engage the flywheel, you may be able to shim the starter so it will work temporarily.

Cut a thin piece of paper or cardboard to insert under the side of the starter toward the engine block. This makeshift shim will serve to cant the starter gear toward the flywheel, thereby engaging the gears deeper. Be careful when you first try this. A shim that is too thick can make the starter jam in the flywheel. It is better to start with a single thin piece of paper and build up as needed.

Reinstall the starter with the shim and try to start the vehicle. If the starter still fails to engage, it needs a thicker shim. If the starter jams, you need to make the shim thinner.

If you cannot fix the problem using this method and you cannot push-start the vehicle, you will only get the vehicle going by replacing the worn parts.

Bad Starter Motor

If when you bypassed the relay or solenoid, you still could not get the starter to spin, the starter motor may be faulty.

Starters usually fail to turn due to bad brush contacts or a short in the motor windings. Turning the motor as little as one-quarter inch may provide contact on a different part of its coil windings to get the starter spinning. Once the starter begins to spin, it may continue until it stops in the same location again.

Older starters often have an access cover around the end farthest from the engine bell housing, or the starter shaft extends out the end of the housing. If you can turn the starter slightly by removing the dust cover and reaching inside the motor, you may get it to work.

If the situation warrants the time and hassle of a long shot, you may be able to get the starter to function properly by thoroughly cleaning the starter brushes. This will entail removal and disassembly of the starter with only poor odds of correcting the problem.

A sports car I once owned had the unpleasant habit of developing starter failure on a regular basis. After replacing several expensive starters, I discovered that oil dripped from the twin-cam cylinder head directly onto the starter below. Enough oil would leak past the end plate on the starter motor to gum up the brushes and prevent proper contact.

About once a year the starter would refuse to turn. Rather than buy a new one, I would remove it and clean the gunk off the contacts to make it function again. I have since had similar experiences with other vehicles.

If the starter on your vehicle is especially greasy, it may simply need a good cleaning.

Evaluate your situation. If nothing seems to work, it may be a lot easier to leave the vehicle, find your way to the nearest parts store, and return with a new starter.

3

Battery Not Charging

There are only three major components to the charging system of your vehicle: the battery, the alternator, and the voltage regulator.

Nearly all voltage regulators are now solid state and cannot be repaired or adjusted. Some voltage regulators are built into the alternator, reducing the system to only two components. If you have one of these integral designs, check the service manual to see if the voltage regulator can be replaced on the trail.

Compared to charging systems of 20 years ago, those of today are far more reliable. Unlike old mechanical regulators with moving contacts that would burn, corrode, and stick, causing myriad symptoms, the new solid-state variety either works or does not.

An alternator can fail because of worn bearings, brushes, a burned-out diode, or a failed internal regulator. Worn-out bearings and brushes usually make noises before the alternator stops generating, but there is rarely any warning to diode or regulator failure.

The dash instruments will indicate when the battery is discharging and may even help find the problem.

Every ORV should be equipped with an ammeter. If you own a vehicle that simply flashes a little red "idiot light" when something is wrong, I suggest you go to a local auto parts store and invest in an ammeter to mount under the dash. As you go through this chapter you will find that an ammeter is more than a handy dash accessory; it is a useful diagnostic tool that tells you when your engine is discharging, by how much, and what part has failed.

No Charging or Discharge at Idle

Before you do anything else, check the fan belt for proper tension, and wire connections to the battery, alternator, and regulator. A loose fan belt or wire can cause partial or total failure of the charging system.

Many vehicles have fusible links between the alternator and starter relay. If this fuse burns out,

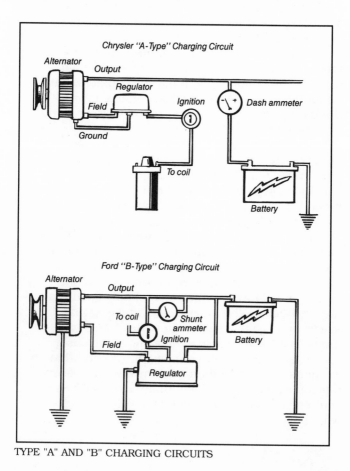

TYPE "A" AND "B" CHARGING CIRCUITS

the alternator field wire will not provide the initial current required to make it operate.

There are two basic alternator/regulator designs. With the "A circuit" design used on many Chrysler products, the alternator receives current from the battery and the regulator works by grounding the field windings. On other vehicles, including most Fords, the system design is called a "B circuit" and the regulator controls power to the alternator.

Consult the service manual wiring schematic to determine which field wire is "hot" when the ignition switch is turned on and whether the system is of an "A" or "B" circuit design. The following schematics should help to determine which system your vehicle has.

CONFIRM POWER TO THE SYSTEM

Confirm power at the alternator with a continuity tester. Turn the ignition switch to On and touch the hot terminals with the grounded tester. The tester should always light when you contact the battery "B" or hot field terminal "F." If the tester lights, you have confirmed that all fuses to the alternator are good. If you cannot get the tester to light when touched to the hot terminal(s), there is a blown fuse or break in the wire. Check the fuses and replace as necessary.

If the fuses are all OK but there is no current flow to the field terminal, it is possible to fix the problem on vehicles equipped with an integral alternator and regulator by clipping a test lead directly between the battery and the field terminal. Remove the wire when the vehicle is turned off to prevent battery discharge. If providing power directly to the alternator did not fix the problem, the alternator or internal regulator has probably failed and will need to be replaced.

If your vehicle has an external voltage regulator

and there is no current at the alternator field
terminal with ignition turned to On, confirm power
to the ignition terminal on the regulator. Lack of
current here will prevent the voltage regulator from
functioning. Check all the fuses and replace as
necessary. Again, you can use a test lead to provide temporary current directly from the battery.

TEST REGULATOR AND ALTERNATOR

If you have checked the wiring but the vehicle is
still discharging, use the following tests to find out
which component has failed. Rev the engine to see
if the ammeter needle will move toward the "charge"
side of the gauge. If the ammeter indicates a
positive charge when the engine is revved, then you
have reason to believe the alternator is generating
output but the voltage regulator has failed.

On "B" circuit systems you can determine
whether the regulator has failed using the following
test. Unplug the voltage regulator. Start the engine
and **quickly** apply battery current to the regulator
field terminal. When power from the battery is applied, it will simulate a working regulator and the
dash instruments will indicate maximum charging.
On "A" circuit systems, connecting a ground wire in
the same way may force the alternator to charge.

If the system does not indicate any charging,
the alternator has probably failed. If dash instruments show the system is charging when the
regulator is bypassed, then you have confirmed the
regulator has failed.

If the regulator is an old mechanical type, a
good wrap may dislodge stuck contacts. If it has a
removable cover, consult your manual for adjustment and repair of the unit.

You should always carry a spare voltage regulator. A voltage regulator can cost less than $10 at
the local parts store, takes only the space of two
cigarette packs, and is easily installed. Replace the

voltage regulator or alternator to correct the problem.

A good battery will recharge itself slightly if allowed to rest for a while. Even if the charging system is inoperative, once the vehicle is started it may run for several miles before there is not enough current to run the ignition. You can extend the usefulness of the battery by removing all the fuses to brake lights (if off road) and accessories.

Consider your options for reaching help when the battery is completely drained and the vehicle will not start.

BATTERY DRAINS OR SEEMS LOW AFTER PARKING

If the engine of the vehicle turns over slowly after it has been parked for a while, and you have checked the battery connections and fan belt as instructed earlier, your vehicle may have a short circuit draining the battery or an ignition timing that is too advanced.

You can confirm that a short circuit is causing battery drain with the following test. Simply operate the vehicle until the battery is fully charged and the vehicle starts easily. Disconnect the battery cables while it is parked. If a short was causing the problem, the vehicle will always start easily after the battery is reconnected.

You may be able to locate the short using the following method.

Turn the ignition switch off and remove the key. Remove all fuses from the main fuse block. With the ground cable connected to the battery, touch the positive (+) battery terminal with the positive (+) cable. Observe closely for sparks as contact is made.

If you have a side-post battery and it is difficult to see the point of contact, use a test lead attached to the cable to touch the terminal.

Since all the major circuits in your vehicle have been disconnected at the fuse block, there should not be a spark upon contact. Begin replacing fuses one at a time. As each fuse is installed, check again at the positive battery terminal for a spark. If you detect a spark, this circuit is using battery current when you are parked. Accessories such as clocks and radios with memories draw small amounts of current all the time. These devices will be on a circuit that will spark; if you are in doubt, simply leave the fuse out of any questionable circuit.

If the problem persists even when you have been disconnecting the battery, the timing may be too far advanced.

Remove the distributor cap and inspect the vacuum advance mechanism to ensure that it is not sticking. Apply mouth suction to the vacuum line

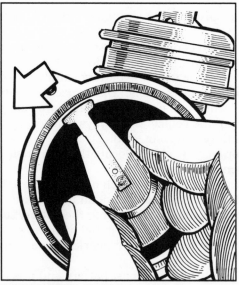

CHECK TIMING ADVANCE

going to it. The distributor plate should move to the advanced position and immediately return when vacuum is released.

If the timing advance mechanism is sticking, you can use carburetor cleaner, starting fluid, or light oil to help free it. Make sure the distributor has dried before you replace the cap and start the vehicle, if you used a combustible fluid.

4

Engine Overheating

If your gauge indicates the engine is overheating or you see steam escaping from under the hood, stop your vehicle immediately and inspect the engine compartment for visible signs of coolant fluid loss. The area near a leak will often not be wet but may be stained from residue left as the coolant evaporated.

Do not remove the radiator cap to determine if the vehicle is overheated.

Most new vehicles have a normal operating temperature just under the boiling point. When you stop the engine, you also stop coolant flow through the hot engine block. Even at normal operating temperatures coolant in the engine block may boil without pressure to contain it. When you remove the radiator cap you allow the coolant to boil. Not only will you risk getting scalded and losing fluid but you will never be able to determine whether a low coolant level caused the overheating.

Before you use the last of your water supply to fill the radiator, be certain that the vehicle will carry you and your passengers to safety. If you doubt the prospect of a successful repair, do not use the last of your water. Water may be required to ensure survival of your party.

Fluid Loss from Cooling System

Release pressure on the system when it is safe. This will help prevent coolant from escaping. Because antifreeze is a much more efficient coolant than water, try to capture escaping coolant for reuse. Dirty coolant should be strained through a piece of cloth when it is poured back into the radiator.

A small crack in a metal part can be temporarily repaired with one of many radiator leak sealant products.

Sealant products will stop small leaks most quickly if there is slight pressure on the system to force the active ingredients into the crack. Read the instructions on the container. Most products indicate the minimum time an engine should run with pressure on the cooling system to seal a leak.

When the engine has cooled so it will accept water without boiling, add the sealant, top off the radiator, and refit the cap. Run the engine at idle for the instructed amount of time while observing the leak. An occasional revving of the engine will help the sealant circulate. When the leak has stopped, you should be able to drive.

If you are concerned that the leak may be too large for the sealant to hold or if the radiator begins leaking again after you have driven a short distance, try loosening the radiator cap and driving without pressure on the system

If the leak does not stop, the hole may be too large for the additive to plug. See "Repairing Radiator Leaks or Punctures," below.

Once the leak has been temporarily repaired, you should be able to proceed. Watch the temperature gauge closely so you will know if the leak does not stay fixed.

REPAIRING HOSE RUPTURE

While radiator sealant products work for temporary radiator, freeze plug, or water pump repairs, they will rarely seal hose ruptures.

Hoses often fail at the clamp ends, so if they are long enough, they can be cut and reclamped to fix the leak. If you are prepared and carry extra hose material, replace the bad hose. If you are not prepared, a hose can be temporarily repaired with duct tape. Try to dry the area before wrapping the duct tape. This action will help it seal.

Drive the vehicle with the radiator cap loose so there is minimal pressure in the system. This will help the makeshift repair last until the hose can be replaced.

REPAIRING RADIATOR LEAKS OR PUNCTURES

Radiator punctures are easily repaired if you have the right material. Unlike a split seam or minor corrosion problem that can be fixed with sealant, a puncture usually leaves a large hole that does not seal with liquid sealant products.

If the puncture is in the core of the radiator and not in the tanks at the top or bottom, you may be able to fix it by crimping the leaking tube with needle-nose pliers and adding sealant to the radiator. Do not be concerned about damage to the radiator. The core will have to be replaced anyway for a good permanent repair. Just be careful not to add more holes to the tubes on either side or to the row of tubes behind the puncture.

Epoxy glue can be applied around the puncture if you want a stronger repair. I do not recommend using epoxy for permanent radiator repairs, but it does work and will get you home.

Epoxy will seal nearly any radiator leak if the area is clean and dry when applied. A squirt of starting fluid makes a good volatile solvent with which to remove anti-freeze residue and dirt.

Drive the vehicle with the radiator cap loose so the cooling system will not pressurize and renew the leak.

No Sign of Fluid Loss

The "idiot lights" and gauges provided as standard equipment on most vehicles are notoriously inaccurate and can provide a false reading.

Feel the top of the radiator and other areas around the engine. Listen for the sound of hot metal and boiling. An overheated engine often ticks and makes strange gurgling noises if it has heated beyond the normal operating temperature. Also, a hot engine will give off a smell, even if there is no coolant escaping. Normal grease buildup on the

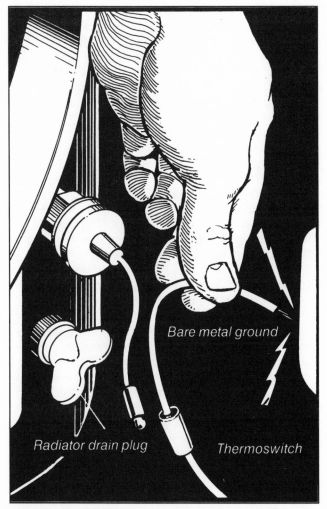

Bare metal ground

Radiator drain plug

Thermoswitch

BYPASSING FAN SWITCH

engine, paint, and wiring will fume as if it were being baked.

Check the front of the radiator for foreign material that may block airflow through the radiator
core, and clean as necessary.

Check the fan belts to ensure that they have not
broken or loosened, and replace or tighten as necessary. If your vehicle has several belts of different
lengths, a universal emergency fan belt is a convenient item to carry. You simply cut one of these
belts to the right length and bolt it together.

If your vehicle has an auxiliary electric fan, the
fan should turn on when the engine heats beyond
normal operating temperature. If it does not turn
on, the engine can overheat. The thermostatic fan
switch located near the bottom of the radiator is
probably not functioning.

The thermostatic switch will have one or two
wires connected to it. Attach the wires together or
the single wire to a nearby ground. The fan will
turn on immediately when the engine is started and
will run continuously to help cooling.

Old hoses sometimes get soft, and the wire
support inside rusts away. Inspect the lower radiator hose to see if it collapses when the engine is
revved. The hose should remain round and firm as
the engine is revved. If it does not, water pump
suction is collapsing the hose and restricting coolant flow to cause the overheating. Either replace
the hose or wrap it with duct tape for reinforcement.
If you can keep the hose from collapsing, the engine
should not overheat.

Check the engine oil. If the oil level is low, the
engine will run hotter, even though there is oil
pressure. Oil not only is a lubricant, but also helps
transfer heat energy created by the friction of
moving parts through the engine block to the coolant. Review the section on oil pressure loss for
more information.

FAULTY TEMPERATURE GAUGE

Inspect the overflow bottle near the radiator to see whether it has filled above the normal operating temperature capacity line.

If the overflow bottle is not fuller than normal and there are none of the telltale signs of overheating, your vehicle may have a bad gauge or temperature sensor. This is particularly probable if the temperature gauge pegged all the way to the hot side. A gauge that slowly moves into the hot range is more credible.

After the engine has been turned off a short while, turn the ignition switch so the instruments work. If the temperature gauge is accurate, it should move farther into the hot range as heat from the cylinders dissipates into the engine block.

When I first purchased my Dodge pickup, the temperature gauge would periodically provide false readings. I would turn a corner and suddenly the gauge would "peg" on the hot side.

I eventually determined that the clip fastened to the sending unit was grounding on the sender case. I pushed the clip further into its rubber housing and have not had a problem since.

While off road in remote areas, you should always double-check a gauge that indicates severe overheating. If you have the same experience I did but do not check it out, you could waste a lot of time or money when nothing is really wrong.

If you suspect that the gauge may not be working properly, turn the ignition switch so the dash instruments are on. Locate the sending unit. Remove the wire from the top of the sending unit and touch it to a convenient ground on the engine block. When the wire is removed, the gauge should go to the cold side of the scale, and when it is grounded it should move all the way to the "hot" side.

Even if there are no conclusive signs of over-heating, let the engine cool down before you inspect the coolant level. If the engine has been running at normal operating temperature, it should only take 15 to 30 minutes to cool.

Loosen but do not remove the radiator cap to re-lease pressure in the system.

When the pressure is released, carefully remove the radiator cap and inspect the coolant level. If it appears full, start the engine and run it a short while with the cap off to ensure that the engine block is full. Top off the radiator as necessary.

Be careful! If the engine has overheated, coolant entering a hot block can immediately boil, causing fluid to shoot out of the radiator.

If the coolant level is normal, you can be certain the engine's temperature was not high enough to cause serious damage. An engine that is severely overheated will boil coolant past the pressure relief spring in the cap.

If you cannot find a leak in the system and the fluid level was only slightly below normal, simply topping off the radiator may fix the problem. Some newer vehicles are designed with barely enough radiator area to cool the engine in hot climates or at slow off-road speeds. Even a slightly low radiator can cause overheating. These vehicles will often operate at a safe temperature when filled to ca-pacity.

In addition to keeping an eye on the gauge, you may want to run the vehicle in a different RPM range or to turn on the heater. If you have been going slowly, more RPMs may circulate added coolant and improve the fan airflow through the radiator. Turning the heater on is like adding another square foot of radiator and will help lower the engine operating temperature several degrees.

STUCK THERMOSTAT

If the problem continues and you cannot keep the vehicle in a safe operating range, you may have a stuck thermostat. A properly functioning thermostat does not help cool your engine; just the opposite. The thermostat restricts coolant flow into the engine block from the radiator. The thermostat forces the engine to warm up quickly and maintains a predetermined high operating temperature which reduces exhaust emissions.

A faulty thermostat may not cause the engine to immediately overheat. An overheating problem caused by a faulty thermostat may develop gradually over hours or weeks of driving.

One of my cars gradually ran hotter over the course of about a year. It never overheated to the boiling point, but the operating temperature of the engine steadily increased until the auxiliary electric fan continued to run every time it warmed up.

When I replaced the thermostat, the car ran a full 20 degrees cooler and the auxiliary fan quit running.

Be aware that a thermostat that only opens part way may contribute to the overheating you believe is caused by hot weather or hard-going off-road terrain.

If your radiator fill cap is on the top of the radiator, you will be able to determine whether the thermostat is opening. Let the engine cool all the way down to air temperature.

Remove the radiator cap, fill the radiator, and, with the engine idling, watch the top of the coolant in the radiator. There should be no circulation of the water until the engine warms up to operating temperature. When the engine warms and the thermostat opens, you will be able to see coolant circulate. When the engine is revved, the coolant level should be sucked lower, and it will be obvious when the thermostat is opened.

If you cannot see circulation of coolant in the radiator after the engine warms to operating temperature, you know the thermostat is sticking. There is a remote chance that a good hard wrap to the thermostat housing may loosen it, but it may stick again. If you have water to refill the radiator, removing the thermostat should solve the problem. It is not needed for safe operation of most vehicles.

Removing the thermostat may cause you to lose most of the coolant. Consult your service manual if you have never removed your thermostat and do not know how much coolant will be lost.

If you do not have water with you, it may be better to stop periodically and allow the engine to cool rather than attempt removal of the thermostat.

INTAKE MANIFOLD VACUUM LEAKS

Intake manifold leaks cause a lean fuel mixture, which will make the engine lose power and run hot.

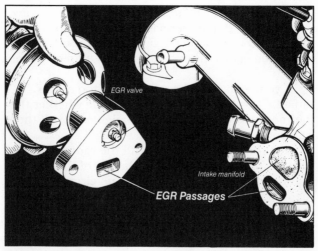

EGR VALVE

When the engine has cooled, open the hood and listen for whistling sounds as the engine idles. If the sound is caused by a vacuum leak, it will disappear when the throttle is depressed and manifold vacuum drops. If you hear a questionable sound, tighten all accessible manifold bolts and plug leaking vacuum hoses.

If the vehicle has an emission gas recirculation (EGR) valve, confirm that it is functioning properly. The EGR valve adds air to the intake manifold as part of the emission system for more complete fuel combustion. Your service manual should provide a detailed explanation of its function and operation. If the valve is leaking around the base gasket or stuck open, it will cause a lean fuel mixture and your engine will run hot. Depending on the design of your emission system, the EGR may be vacuum actuated; if it is, suspicious functioning may be prevented by blocking the vacuum line so the valve stays closed.

Last summer friends and I were on our way to the eastern Sierras in my 3/4 Dodge pickup when it started to heat up on a steep, narrow, canyon road.

I had just had the vehicle smog inspected, and the mechanic had replaced the EGR valve. He had trouble getting the valve to seal on the intake manifold and used two gaskets that were not metal-impregnated asbestos. Heat from the engine caused the gaskets to shrink until they leaked and blew out. The engine overheated, lost power, and stopped.

We were stranded in the dark on a dirt road at 8,000 feet, with a howling cold wind and no help. I removed the valve, fashioned a gasket from a beer can and that did the trick. We managed to get to the top of the pass where we spent the night, and then made repairs the next day.

These gaskets will fail due to old age and can

easily strand ORVs. If you live in an area that does not require regular mandatory smog inspection, you should inspect the condition of the EGR valve gasket as part of regular preventive maintenance.

5

Low Oil Pressure

Few problems can cause as much damage to an engine as prolonged operation without oil pressure.

I have a relative who went shopping in the family car. When she stopped for gas, the station attendant checked the oil (the arcane custom of the day) and proclaimed, "Lady, you haven't a drop of oil in your engine. You want me to fill it up?" She replied, "No, I think my husband has some at home in the garage." Unfortunately it was 25 miles back to the garage. When the car was turned off, it dieseled for a while and never ran again.

To this day she insists, "The indicator light didn't come on, and the car didn't make any noises."

Running an engine dry will quickly ruin the whole engine block. My relative's car engine would not even turn over, because once the engine cooled the piston rods, crank shaft, and block became one solid welded unit.

Do not attempt to drive your vehicle out of remote areas without lubrication oil in the engine. If you do, be aware that you may need to buy a new engine if you ever reach your destination.

If your oil is low, it will first become evident when you are going up a hill or around a corner. A good gauge or indicator light will show temporary pressure reductions as soon as the oil pump "sucks air." Pressure will go back up when the oil flows back to the center of the oil pan.

Whenever your instruments indicate low oil pressure, stop immediately and turn the engine off. Check the oil level. If the oil level is low, inspect the engine for serious oil leaks. Leaks from valve covers, oil filters, or other parts can often be stopped by tightening the part.

If there is almost no oil in the engine, look for a severe leak. Check the oil pan for punctures or gasket leaks.

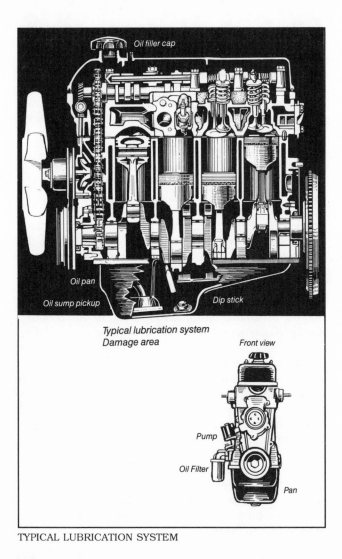

TYPICAL LUBRICATION SYSTEM

Unusual Oil Consumption

If you checked the oil before leaving home and now it is just below the minimum mark on the dipstick, driving conditions may have increased oil consumption. Older vehicles will consume more oil when driven over rough terrain with the engine providing the braking resistance down steep grades.

If your inspection of the engine reveals no punctures or serious leaks, do not be concerned. Top off the oil level and proceed with caution.

Engine Oil Pan Punctures

The sudden loss of oil while driving off road is usually caused by a puncture in the oil pan. Should this happen and you have epoxy glue or putty with you, it can be easily fixed at the edge of the trail.

Drain any oil remaining in the engine into a clean container so it can be reused. Use a screwdriver or other tools to bend the pan back to near original shape. This can usually be done without removing it from the engine. Clean the area to be repaired with gasoline and then starting fluid.

When the area around the puncture is clean of oil and has dried, knead the epoxy putty as instructed on the package and press the putty firmly into the puncture. A coating of liquid epoxy over the putty and surrounding area will help seal the puncture further. Providing the area was clean and dry when the epoxy was applied and it is allowed to set firmly before you add the oil, the seal should last until you find permanent repairs.

If you lost all the oil in the pan and do not have 4 quarts of motor oil, you can use automatic transmission fluid to fill the engine. **Do not use more than 50 percent ATF.**

If you use ATF to "top off" the oil level, be sure

not to place the engine under heavy load. ATF is less viscous than regular motor oil and does not have the same lubrication properties. As long as you take it easy and watch both the temperature and oil pressure, you should be able to reach a location where the ATF/motor oil mixture can be replaced.

OIL LEVEL NORMAL

If the oil level is within the marks on the dipstick, but the gauge or warning light indicates a total loss of oil pressure, the oil pump may have failed.

It is easy to determine whether the engine has oil pressure. Loosen or remove the oil filter. If you do not have a filter wrench, you should be able to loosen it with a rag and firm grip. Start the engine briefly. If the pump is working, oil will squirt from the engine block. If no oil squirts from the block, then the oil pump has failed and you should not start or drive the vehicle.

If the oil level is OK and oil squirts from around the filter, you should be able to continue on your way safely despite the reading on the gauge or indicator light. Do not forget to tighten the oil filter before you drive off. As an added precaution, continue to listen for unusual noises and watch the engine temperature as you drive.

If oil does not squirt from the filter base, the oil pump has stripped. Unless your vehicle has an external oil pump and you have a spare, there is no way to correct the problem.

6

Brake Failure

Driving off road can be harder on brakes than road racing. Off-road terrain requires the brakes to be applied for extended periods without the benefit of high-speed wind turbulence for cooling.

Heat generated at the brakes will vaporize any water in the brake fluid (which always settles closest to the heat source). When this happens, your brake lines fill with air bubbles.

Some car manufacturers recommend the use of silicone, rather than petroleum-based brake fluid. Or, they suggest, you should completely replace the petroleum brake fluid every six months. Silicone fluid does not absorb moisture from the air and helps prevent "spongy" or "pulling" brake symptoms. Silicone fluid is more expensive. If you are like most people and brake service simply means topping off the reservoir, silicone fluid may reduce the incidence of brake fade caused by water condensation.

Even if you use silicone fluid, water can still get into the brakes when you ford streams or drive in heavy rains. Even if you use silicone brake fluid, you should bleed the brakes at least once a year to ensure that the wheel cylinders do not rust.

If the brakes are spongy, pull in one direction, or seem as if they do not stop the way they should, check the fluid level in the brake reservoir.

Inspect the drums or rotors to see whether they are hot by feeling the center of your wheels. **Be careful. A hot brake drum can burn your hand.** Hot brakes also have a distinctive smell.

If the fluid is not low and the brakes are HOT-HOT-HOT, they may just need a chance to cool off. The material used in most brake linings will glaze slightly if heated but quickly wear to a good gripping surface again when cool.

If the fluid is low, check the inside of each wheel for signs of a leaking brake cylinder. **If your vehicle**

**has been parked for a while in snake country, be
careful to check for any snakes that may have decided to nap under your vehicle.**

If you have discovered a leaking drum brake
cylinder, you may be able to reduce fluid loss by
adjusting the brake shoes. Changing brake adjustment will move the seals inside the cylinder to a
new location and may stop the leak until repairs can
be made.

Most vehicles are equipped with a split master
cylinder, so even if you lose braking on the front or
back, partial braking will be maintained. If you keep
the brake reservoir filled, you will have at least
partial braking.

If you find yourself in a survival situation without
brakes on your vehicle due to fluid loss and the
terrain requires better braking than the emergency
brake can provide, there is still one option. You can
use water as emergency brake fluid. Water has low
enough viscosity to work the hydraulics. Water is

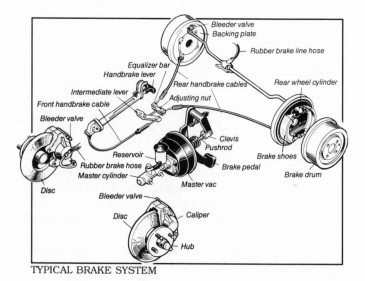

TYPICAL BRAKE SYSTEM

usually more plentiful than brake fluid and may provide a better alternative than proceeding without brakes. Unfortunately, as discussed earlier, water will vaporize easily, and any hard application of the brakes can result in their failure to stop the vehicle. Obviously, you will need to remove the water from the brake system as soon as possible to prevent corrosion in the system.

You should use water in the brakes only as a means of survival. Proceed with extreme caution, assuming the brakes will not work on demand, and use the emergency brake as backup. Do not attempt any terrain where the emergency brake would be inadequate.

The last section of this book contains a true story about the

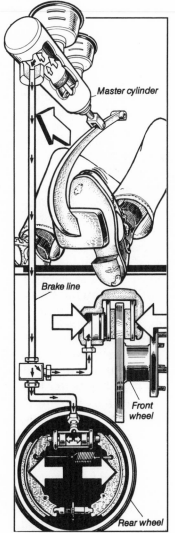

Master cylinder

Brake line

Front wheel

Rear wheel

HYDRAULIC BRAKE SYSTEM

danger of driving without brakes. Before you go anywhere without brakes make sure it is absolutely necessary and that other alternatives are not acceptable.

7

Flat Tires

PUNCTURES

The best protection against stranding because of a flat tire is a good spare and jack. This should cover 99 percent of the circumstances the typical off-roader encounters, but there are times when you would prefer an alternative to changing a tire.

Many off-roaders have "giant meats on all fours" but an original size tire for the spare. Even two inches in diameter can ruin traction and handling, not to mention aesthetics.

On several occasions I have stumbled upon un-fortunates with flat tires, no air in the spare, and the same wheel bolt pattern as my vehicle. It always seems as if I am loaning a perfect stranger my own security in the form of a spare after he has shown total disregard for his own.

Also, if you have ever changed an inside dual tire on a large RV or one-ton pickup, you know it can be a real hassle.

In these situations a can of inflater/sealer and a puncture repair kit can make permanent repairs in under 15 minutes without removing the tire.

I have had better luck with the impregnated-cord type puncture kits than the solid rubber. The cord helps the plug remain intact as it is pushed into the tire and keeps it there when the insertion tool is withdrawn from the hole.

Some inexpensive repair kits do not work well because the tool provided to insert the plug bends or breaks off in an 8-ply rated truck radial. If the tool works correctly, it should hook over the plug and slide into the puncture. When the tool is removed, a slot in the tip will allow the tool to be withdrawn, leaving the plug deep in the tire.

Most auto parts stores sell a professional T-handle tire repair kit that is superior to inex-pensive kits. The T-handle makes insertion of a

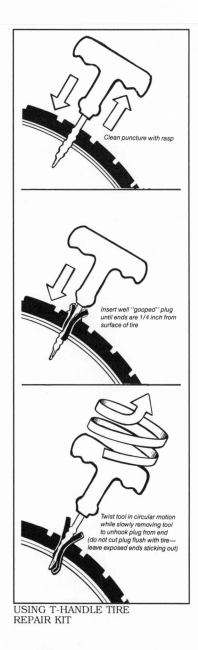

Clean puncture with rasp

Insert well "gooped" plug until ends are 1/4 inch from surface of tire

Twist tool in circular motion while slowly removing tool to unhook plug from end (do not cut plug flush with tire— leave exposed ends sticking out)

USING T-HANDLE TIRE
REPAIR KIT

plug in 8-ply radial tires easier, and heavier con-
struction reduces the chance of breaking the tool
off inside the tire.

If you want to be doubly sure a plugged puncture will not leak again, have the tire patched when
you return to civilization.

TORN VALVE STEMS

One of the first accessories off-roaders buy for their
4 X 4 is fancy aftermarket wheels. Some people
will remove the hubcaps to change the look of a
rig, believing they are only cosmetic. They could
not be more wrong. Hubcaps may protect the valve
stems from damage.

A basketball-sized rock can flip over into the
wheels and damage the exposed valve stem. A
good wheel will be designed so the valve stem is
tucked toward its center or protected by a hubcap.

My Dodge pickup has stock 16.5-inch rims and
truck hubcaps. While they do not look fancy, a
rock large enough to cause any damage to the stem
is held away by the protruding hubcap.

Before you buy fancy "street" wheels for your
ORV, ask to see how the hub covers and valve
stems fit in the rims. This will be a good test of
whether the rims are truly intended for off-road
use.

Experienced off-roaders replace valve stems
several times during the life of a tire to ensure they
remain flexible and tear resistant. It is convenient
and less expensive if this is done when you have
the tires rotated and balanced.

If you experience a flat caused by a torn valve
stem, you should change to the spare. If for some
reason the spare is not usable, you may be able to
fix the stem without removing the wheel and tire.
Five-minute epoxy will temporarily repair the stem

until permanent repairs can be made. Once the stem has been glued it can be easily damaged again. Most tire inflator/sealer cans have a screw-on hose. A portable 12-volt tire pump with a clip-on hose will fill the tire with less chance of re-breaking the stem.

JACKING VEHICLE

It is always safest to find a flat hard area in which to make a tire change, but that is not always possible if you want to avoid damage to the tire and rim.

Some light-duty four-wheel-drive vehicles are only equipped with bumper jacks. If you are not sure what kind of jack is in your vehicle, you had better take a look before you find yourself in a fix, cursing the manufacturer.

Bumper jacks are less stable than those that provide lift directly under the axle or suspension, especially on sand or slopes. While bumper jacks are more convenient, they should not be relied on for changing tires off road. A bumper jack must raise the body off the suspension before the tire is lifted from the ground. Depending on the suspension travel of the vehicle, it may require lifting the

Place large block under
jack to distribute load

Block wheels
Place in park or gear
Engage emergency brake

SAFE JACKING TECHNIQUE ON SOFT GROUND

Dig out level areas in the hillside for wheels and jack
Always have flat on downhill side—so you jack the vehicle uphill
Make sure jack is on a stable block to distribute side forces.
Do not put blocks on top of jack.
Block wheels with rocks; engage emergency brake; place in Park

SAFE JACKING TECHNIQUE ON HILLSIDE

vehicle a foot or more. This is obviously not prefer-
able for safe hillside tire changes. In contrast, a
hydraulic or screw jack properly placed under the
axle or suspension will usually free a tire with only 2
to 3 inches of lift.

If you cannot reach a safe flat area, park on the
hill with the flat tire on the uphill side. In this way a
sliding vehicle will move away from you. Always
block the tires on the downhill side with rocks or
wood.

If the hill is extremely steep and you are concerned that the vehicle may roll or slide, consider
removing dirt from under the tire rather than jacking

it. Use your jack to raise the axle enough to slide a
large rock or log underneath for added support.
When the axle is supported, you will be able to
remove dirt from under the tire while the vehicle
remains stable. Once the tire is changed, replace as
much of the dirt as possible, remove the rocks or log,
and drive away.

Another common problem is ground that is too
soft to support a jack base. If you cannot jack the
axle, then digging under the tire will not work either.

First, try to distribute the jack load with a large
flat rock or any other material. Even carpet, grass,
or brush will help support the jack. Have a large
solid object ready to wedge under the axle for more
support. If this does not work, there is still one more
option. The following jacking method may work if
you own a well-designed vehicle without exposed
wires or brake lines under the axle housing.

Stout log

Rock

Dig dirt out from under tire for fender clearance if needed
Drive up log so it slides under axle without damaging vehicle and supports weight

Block wheels—put vehicle in park or gear with emergency brake engaged

MAKESHIFT LOG JACK

If you are in a wooded area, lean a large straight log (8 to 10 inches in diameter and 4 to 5 feet long) against a boulder. Slowly drive the vehicle up the log, so that the log slides under the axle housing and lifts the appropriate wheel off the ground.

The vehicle may need assistance getting back off the log if a rear-drive wheel is being changed. Two-wheel-drive vehicles without limited slip differentials will spin the high wheel and may need to be pushed off the log. Rear-wheel changes on 4-wheel-drives should be no problem if you apply the parking brake to transmit drive to the front wheels.

If you are in a nonwooded area, you may be able to execute the same idea with an appropriately shaped boulder or stack of boulders, but at greater risk of damage to your vehicle.

8

Driveline Failure

Most serious driveline failures develop slowly over hundreds of miles with telltale noises and progressive deterioration. These conditions should be repaired before the vehicle ventures off road.

"Clunk" sounds when shifting from forward gears to reverse often indicate that the drive shaft universal joints are starting to wear out. Automatic transmissions may slip when they get older, especially when starting out on a hill or deep sand.

Universal joints are inexpensive to replace, and automatic transmission slippage can often be corrected with low-cost servicing and adjustment. Either condition can leave an off-roader stranded if left to deteriorate until the part fails.

Some noises, inherent in particular makes, are less cause for concern. Many Chrysler products manufactured in the late 1970s and early 1980s have an inordinate amount of play in the rear axle differential. The annoying "clunk" sounds as if the driveline is ready to fall out, but represents minimal risk of failure.

If you are not sure whether driveline noises are

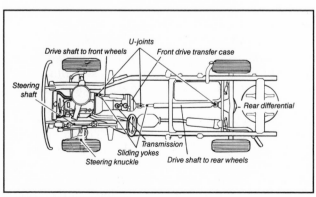

TYPICAL 4WD DRIVELINE

serious, have the vehicle inspected by a professional mechanic.

You can inspect universal joints yourself. Place the vehicle in Neutral with the parking brake engaged. With the vehicle safely jacked up, twist on the drive shaft and watch for play. It is normal for the drive shaft to have play at the rear end and transmission, but the universal joints should be tight, allowing no rotational movement within the joint. If there is even the slightest movement within a universal joint, it should be replaced.

Engine Runs, Vehicle Fails to Move

AUTOMATIC TRANSMISSION

If the vehicle makes loud grinding noises when placed in drive, the transmission or differential is probably broken internally and there is little chance of repair on the trail. You are not likely to cause much more damage by trying to limp to help.

I once owned a GMC van that started developing transmission slippage at 90,000 miles. On the day I was leaving for a one-week vacation, the transmission failed. As it shifted between first and second gear there was a loud "crunch," then grinding, and the engine ran free as if in neutral.

I pulled to the side of the road and got out to see if the transmission case had split and spilled oil on the road. When I saw the case was still intact, I started the engine and put it in gear to see if it would roll.

The van would not work in drive, but when shifted manually drove with a lot of crunching and funny noise. I was surprised after all the horrible noises the van would go ten miles through city traffic and a dozen stop lights back to the repair garage.

If the automatic transmission fails off road and you can get the vehicle moving, you might as well get all the distance out of it you can. The transmission may go 10 or 20 miles closer to help, and it is doubtful that you will add much to the repair cost.

If there was no noise from the transmission, inspect the transmission fluid level. Check the fluid to see if it smells burned, and inspect the dipstick for varnish buildup or "junk" sticking to it. These are all signs of a tired, slipping transmission.

If the transmission fluid is low, inspect the bottom of the transmission for punctures and leaks. Punctures can be repaired in the same manner as described for oil-pan punctures (see "Low Oil Pressure," chap. 5). Leaks around the oil-pan gasket can often be stopped by tightening the bolts.

My Dodge pickup once developed a transmission-pan gasket leak so severe that the only way to repair it was to remove the pan and replace the gasket with silicone sealer. Silicone sealer will make a good temporary gasket if it is applied thickly and allowed to dry completely before the pan is reinstalled.

Do not be tempted to fill the transmission with motor oil. Motor oil will cause permanent damage to the transmission and will probably not allow you to drive far before it stops working.

If the fluid level in the transmission is normal, inspect the transmission shift linkage located on the side of the transmission. If linkage levers have fallen off, the vehicle may not shift the transmission into drive. Refit the linkage to its original location, and it should again shift into drive.

An improperly adjusted linkage will also prevent the transmission from shifting or engaging. Start the vehicle and slowly shift between gears. If you can feel the transmission engage when the shift lever is between gears as indicated on the dash, you know the linkage has been bent or has come out of proper adjustment. Consult you service manual for the proper adjustment of the shift linkage, and repair as necessary.

If the transmission fluid level is normal and there appears to be no malfunction of the transmission linkage, consult your service manual for the location of band adjustment bolts. On many transmissions, the first and reverse gear band adjustments are located inside the transmission body and are not easily accessible. But if your transmission has an external adjustment for first gear, you might try tightening the band to eliminate slippage.

If the vehicle will move in reverse but not in a forward gear, you can try backing up a small hill. The assistance from gravity or a push start may help. Once rolling, there may be enough friction in the first gear transmission band to build speed so the transmission will shift into second. Once the transmission has shifted into second, it may operate without slipping. If you can sustain this speed, you may be able to drive the vehicle.

Consider your options for getting help if none of these suggestions corrects the failure to drive.

MANUAL TRANSMISSION VEHICLES

A manual transmission failure that develops quickly, without warning, is probably caused by a broken clutch or gearbox.

Manual gearboxes are extremely reliable. If one gear fails to work, you will usually be able to use another to drive the vehicle. Even if the case of a manual transmission is cracked so the gear oil leaks out, it will continue to function. When a gear box is cracked, you can temporarily repair the damage using the same technique described for repairing oil pan punctures. Any type of oil you have available to fill the gearbox will be better than running the transmission without lubricant.

If you experience the rare occasion when a manual gearbox fails, there is little you can do to correct the problem at the edge of the trail.

The clutch is the part of the manual transmission driveline most susceptible to wear. Under normal circumstances, a clutch will wear until it slips or makes loud noises.

Screeching noises when the clutch pedal is depressed usually indicates a bad throwout or pilot bearing. The sound often goes away when the clutch is released, and the bad bearing rarely causes additional damage to the vehicle if driven.

If the clutch has been allowed to wear until it will no longer engage, the condition may not be reparable on the trail. If the route out of the area is relatively flat so speed can be maintained, you may be able to push-start the vehicle or coast down a hill to get underway. Sometimes a badly worn clutch has enough friction to maintain the momentum of the vehicle once it has started rolling.

If none of these methods seems to work, consider your options for reaching help.

DRIVE SHAFT FAILURE

Most experienced off-roaders will not straddle large objects such as rocks or stumps which pass directly under the engine or exposed driveline components. Most ORVs have little protection under the drive shaft or constant velocity (CV) joints. An exposed drive shaft can bend or a universal joint loosen when smashed against a rock by the weight of the vehicle.

A bent or severely damaged drive shaft will often make the entire vehicle shake at high speeds and may cause damage to other driveline parts. On vehicles equipped with limited slip transfer cases (Jeep Quadratrac™) a damaged drive shaft can be removed and the vehicle driven in four-wheel drive. All power will be delivered to the wheels connected to the engine by a drive shaft.

Removal of the drive shaft is easy and only

involves unbolting the rear flange at the differential
and sliding the shaft off the transmission spline.
Wrap the exposed opening in the transmission with
a rag to prevent dust and dirt from entering the
transmission.

CLUTCH FAILS TO DISENGAGE

This problem can sometimes be corrected at the
edge of the trail through adjustment of the clutch
linkage.

Inspect the tightness of the rod that pushes
against the main clutch lever protruding from the
engine bell housing. You should be able to feel only
slight play when the clutch pedal is up. There may
be spring tension against the linkage, so give it a
good push to see if it is sloppy. Adjust as necessary
to remove the play.

If your vehicle has hydraulic clutch actuation,
verify that the clutch reservoir is filled with brake
fluid. If the fluid is low, inspect the slave cylinder
for visible signs of fluid loss. If the slave cylinder
appears to be leaking, fill the reservoir and bleed
the system to make the clutch disengage. If the
slave cylinder continues to leak profusely when the
clutch pedal is depressed and the rod between the
slave cylinder and clutch lever is adjustable, try
lengthening the rod. Moving the location of the
piston in a worn hydraulic cylinder will often reduce
leakage.

If the fluid level is normal, watch the slave
cylinder as someone presses the clutch pedal.
When the clutch is depressed, you should be able to
see the clutch lever move. If it does not, the master
cylinder is not pumping fluid. Bleed the system to
remove air from the master cylinder. If bleeding or
pumping the clutch pedal does not disengage the
clutch, it is doubtful that you will get the master
cylinder to work properly.

Fluid reservoir

Pushrod free play
adjusting nut

Clutch master
cylinder

Clutch pedal

Adjusting nuts   Clutch slave cylinder

Return spring

Free play   Bleeder valve

HYDRAULIC CLUTCH LINKAGE ADJUSTMENT

A failure of the clutch to disengage can be dangerous in rough terrain. While it is possible to start the vehicle in low and jam the gear box to shift up through gears, without a clutch it is often difficult to downshift when needed most for control on steep grades.

Most vehicles are designed so that about 80 percent of all braking is at the front wheels. This means the front wheels are prone to "locking up" on steep gravel hills when the brakes are applied, causing loss of steering. You may slide out of control unless the vehicle is in a higher gear so the wheels continue to turn.

If your clutch will not disengage so you can put the vehicle in gear when going down a steep gravel hill, use the emergency brake to maintain control. Most emergency brakes only work on the rear wheels. If you depress the emergency brake enough to provide drag in the rear and then brake normally with the pedal, you should be able to maintain better control than freewheeling down the hill.

PART 2

OUTDOOR
SKILLS
AND
SURVIVAL

9

Getting Stuck and Unstuck

There are two types of off-roaders: those who use their vehicle as legitimate transportation and those to whom building a vehicle that will go anywhere is a sport and testing their rig is the sole reason for being off road.

I am a conservationist with a passion for leaving the wilderness the way I found it. This passion is unfortunately not shared by all off-roaders, especially those who use their rigs to destroy the terrain off approved trails.

All it takes is a little willpower to go around the spots that are likely to cause problems, and your chances of getting stuck drop substantially.

Before you venture off pavement, stop at a Forest Service office to ask about road conditions. The rangers will tell you not only how difficult your planned route is but also whether any rock slides or impassable spots have been reported.

After fishing in mountains and prospecting in deserts more than 100 miles from the nearest help, I have never felt a need to invest a great deal in winches and pulling equipment.

Most would argue that a good bumper-mounted winch is a necessity, and I agree that it is a handy item. But if you have not invested in a winch, you can still safely enjoy remote areas.

Reasonable rims with modestly oversized tires, a limited slip differential, some common sense, and $100 worth of materials will get you out of most situations involving mud holes or deep sand.

Local soil conditions and weather will greatly influence your need for more expensive equipment. In the West, rocks, sand, and rough terrain are the greatest threat during most of the year. The higher ground clearance and increased surface area of oversized tires (with a good measure of common sense) will help you avoid getting stuck.

If you have the money to equip your truck with a large winch, do so, but weigh the benefits against other useful accessories you may not have. A spare fuel tank, thicker skid plates, roll bars, or auxiliary lights may also help get you out of a jam or prevent a breakdown.

If you invest in a winch, make sure it is large enough for your vehicle. Most would agree a 6,000-pound winch is minimal for most vehicles, and even higher pull ratings are desirable. Do not simply bolt it up and forget the gear you will need to use it properly. You should also carry a length of cable or chain, some extra pulleys, a clevis, a stake, and a tree protector. A 6,000-pound puller can be useless without additional ground tackle.

I used to carry a lever winch (sometimes called a come-along), a 25-foot length of chain, a three-foot metal stake, a piece of Astro Turf, a high-lift jack, and a two-pound mall.

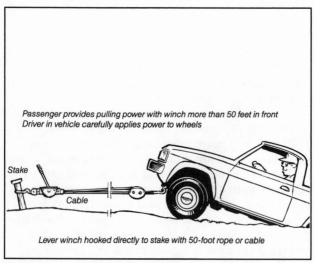

Passenger provides pulling power with winch more than 50 feet in front
Driver in vehicle carefully applies power to wheels

Stake

Cable

Lever winch hooked directly to stake with 50-foot rope or cable

USING LEVER WINCH AND STAKE

If you get stuck, you can simply drive the stake into solid ground, hook the chain and the come-along between the stake and the front bumper, and begin winching. It is less convenient than a bumper-mounted winch but will get you out of a lot of situations without a tow.

I have discovered that a 100-foot length of good pre-stretched sailboat halyard works better than chain. It is lighter, easier to handle, and can be bought in sizes that are just as strong. If you need a tow, braided line has a little stretch to it and will not jerk the frame out from under your vehicle when someone pulls out slack.

A Mohave Desert trail used by amateur prospec-tors crosses several sand-filled washes. On one outing I happened upon a truck equipped with a large winch that could not get through a wash because the owner forgot to bring any ground tackle.

When I began to bog down in the sand, I took out my Astro Turf and laid it green-side down in front of the wheels. I could see the disappointment on the truck driver's face when my $2 solution worked better than his expensive alternative. Of course, he had no choice and borrowed the Astro Turf so he could get through.

A friend who constantly argued against this so-lution begrudgingly admitted to me one day that he had ripped the carpet out of his truck to put under the wheels. I asked why he did not use his winch, and he quietly replied there was not anything to hook onto. Now that the carpet has been replaced in his truck (for about $100), you will always see some of the old carpet behind the seat with a long stout stake and mall.

In most cases, deep sand or mud can be spotted before you enter. Mud under brown sod or frozen soil is the hardest to recognize and can be surprisingly deep if you break through. It is best to skirt the edge of questionable spots or test them first with a stick or your metal stake. Sand or mud will be thinner at the edge of a valley or outside of bends in a wash.

A short walk through questionable areas will divulge the best route. Tracks left by other vehicles are often not a good indication of the safest crossing; they may only indicate the most direct route when conditions were better.

In the early Arizona spring shortly after buying my first 4X4, two friends and I decided to trek from Flagstaff down to the Verde Hot Springs.

The water level of the Verde River was high from snow run-off, but not as high as we had seen it in earlier weeks. The road to the hot springs ends directly across the river from ruins of an old health spa. To get to the enclosed concrete bathhouse, you must cross the river.

There were about six vehicles at the end of the road. The owners were not interested in driving across the river and smartly chose to park where they were and walk across.

A single Jeep Cherokee sat on the opposite bank near what appeared to be tracks leading from the water, just upstream from a rapids. I decided if he could cross the river here, so could I.

The river was about 50 yards wide. We entered the shallows and proceeded in 4-wheel low gear. The water, at the edge was only about a foot deep and no problem until we approached the main current near the other bank.

The front of the jeep fell into a channel. Water splashed over the hood and up the windshield. We could feel the tires slipping on boulders at least three feet in diameter as opposite corners dipped temporarily under water and then back to the surface. I could feel the current moving us side-

ways toward the rapids every time a tire slipped.

Water rushed in the passenger door, over the transmission hump, and out my side. From this side of the river I could see the water 15 feet downstream was deep enough to roll us over and swallow the jeep.

However, the jeep continued to chug through the channel. After what seemed to be an eternity, the front wheels caught gravel on the side of the river, and we crawled up the bank.

It was dumb luck that I did not lose the jeep down the rapids. The vehicle on the other side had simply parked near old tracks. He crossed the river about 100 yards upstream where the bottom is sandy and water was only six inches deep. The tracks on the opposite bank were made during the previous week when the water level was much lower. I did not take the same route back and learned a valuable lesson. Never use tracks to pick a route unless you know they have been recently made!

When you have picked the safest route across suspicious terrain, concentrate on "setting up" your crossing with the maximum safe speed and a gear you can stick with.

When you begin to bog down, keep the engine RPMs up to maintain smooth, even power to the wheels. Do not downshift or accelerate sufficiently to spin the wheels.

When the forward movement of the vehicle ceases and the wheels begin to slip, stop the vehicle. You are stuck, and the last thing you want to do is worsen the situation by spinning the tires and digging yourself to China.

When you find yourself stuck in soft sand or mud, the slightest additional tire tread area will help the vehicle pull up to the surface and out. Lowering the tire air pressure will add 15 to 20 percent to the surface of each tire. Multiplied times four, it is like

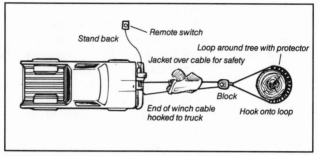

USING BUMPER WINCH AROUND TREE

adding a fifth tire for flotation or traction.

A small portable air compressor is perfect for refilling your tires, but a large can of tire inflator and sealer can refill four small tires if you do not have a compressor.

Place carpet, brush, flat logs, or any material in front of the wheels to help "float" the vehicle or provide traction.

Hook your winch to the nearest solid object, and pull yourself out.

If you have pulling power from a bumper-mounted winch, you should stand back from the vehicle to prevent being injured if the cable breaks. Lay a jacket, heavy blanket, or carpet over the cable for added safety. The weight of the material will help prevent the cable from snapping back into your vehicle.

Never hook the cable from a winch around itself. Always place a loop of cable or chain around the stationary object and hook the winch cable to it. This will prevent damage to the cable and will also allow you to double the pulling power of the winch if you use a snatch block.

Always use a tree protector when hooked around a tree, or pad the cable with carpet and pieces of wood to distribute the load. The cable will dig into

Dig dirt out from front of all wheels so there is gradual slope out to surface

Place carpet, small rocks, or twigs in front of wheels—do not pile higher than bottom of wheels

USING CARPET FOR TRACTION

the tree bark and kill it if you do not. Not only is it poor conservation to kill trees with your winch cable, but in future years the tree will not be there for another off-roader's convenient hookup.

Two people will be required if you are using a small hand winch. Someone will need to drive the vehicle as another provides pull on the winch.

Some areas are notorious for flash floods. When I lived in northern Arizona, an experienced off-roader advised, "When you are near mountains surrounded with rain clouds, stop before crossing a wash and listen for raging water."

I paid attention to his warning and on one occa-sion luckily stopped before crossing a wide wash. I thought I heard something in the distance that sounded like a freight train. Within a few minutes a wall of water about ten feet deep rushed by at amazing speed, carrying trees, brush, and every-thing that it could tear loose.

There is no doubt the water would have caught me in the wash, and I would have been swept away. Within 15 minutes the water was past so I could continue.

In parts of the country that are particularly rocky you will see a high-lift jack tied on the bumper of nearly every 4X4. Even off-roaders with winches value the ability of the "high boy" jack's ability to lift the vehicle over large boulders, often saving damage to the underside.

10

First Aid

EXPOSURE

Most first-aid kits contain instructions for treatment of burns, cuts, abrasions, cardiopulmonary resuscitation (CPR), and for broken bones. Few indicate what to do for the three causes of death from exposure to the elements: heat exhaustion, sunstroke, and hypothermia.

HEAT EXHAUSTION
Many people confuse heat exhaustion and sunstroke. Someone who is suffering from heat exhaustion will become weak and nauseous, complain of

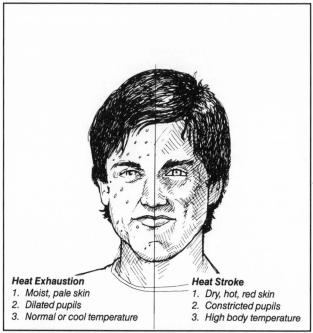

Heat Exhaustion
1. Moist, pale skin
2. Dilated pupils
3. Normal or cool temperature

Heat Stroke
1. Dry, hot, red skin
2. Constricted pupils
3. High body temperature

HEAT EXHAUSTION/SUNSTROKE SYMPTOMS

headaches, and may pass out. Heat exhaustion
often causes severe stomach cramps and vomiting.
The person's skin will appear pale and feel moist
but cool.

Heat exhaustion victims will quickly recover if
laid in the shade with legs elevated, given salt
tablets dissolved in water, and given other non-
alcoholic fluids.

SUNSTROKE

While heat exhaustion is common and only a minor
ailment, sunstroke can be quickly fatal. Even with
prompt treatment, it may take several days for a full
recovery.

The body's heat regulatory system completely
shuts down, and temperature continues to rise until
the person is unconscious, goes into shock, suffers
brain damage, and expires.

The symptoms of sunstroke are strikingly different from heat exhaustion. The person will appear
confused and dizzy, then collapse. The skin will be
dry, hot, and flushed in appearance.

The only treatment for sunstroke is to quickly
lower the person's body temperature. When in a
desert environment lay the individual under shade,
loosen or remove clothing, and fan while sponging
the entire body with water. If a large amount of
water is available, immerse the person completely.

Massage the skin to stimulate circulation.
When the person is fully conscious, have him or her
drink cool liquids.

A person who has suffered sunstroke will recover slowly over 48 hours.

HYPOTHERMIA

The most dangerous condition caused by exposure
to the elements is hypothermia. Unlike victims of
sunstroke or heat exhaustion, victims of hypother-

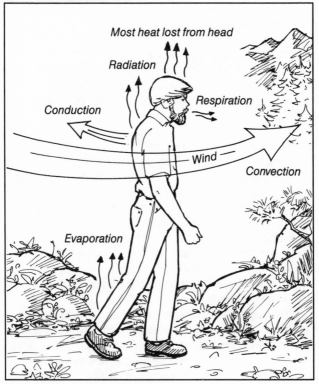

MECHANISMS OF HEAT LOSS

mia are often unaware that they are in danger. The onset of hypothermia is gradual, and victims are usually unaware of their condition, with no sensation of illness.

When a person's temperature begins to drop below 98.6 degrees Fahrenheit (F), they will first begin to shiver from cold discomfort. The shivering will become increasingly intense and eventually uncontrollable. The person will then begin losing mental acuity as oxygen and sugar supplies to the brain are depleted.

At first, the person may simply appear a little dizzy, uncoordinated, and disoriented. The person may stumble, have thick slurred speech and poor judgment, almost as if drunk.

Victims of hypothermia can become euphoric and appear quite comfortable as if the cold does not bother them because their body stops reacting to cold and all sensations are numbed.

In the early stages of hypothermia people often become belligerent. They will insist they feel fine and may not accept help. They may hallucinate and become paranoid. It may be a temptation to let the person wander off or do as he or she wishes, especially if you are also suffering from impaired judgment caused by hypothermia.

Eventually, a victim becomes so sluggish that he or she wants to lie down and go to sleep. The pulse and respiration slow; the heartbeat becomes irregular. Then the victim goes into a coma, and all bodily functions will cease.

The body temperature of someone suffering from hypothermia must be gradually increased. Place the person in a sleeping bag with rocks warmed near a fire and wrapped in dry clothing or towels. In an emergency, when no other source of heat is available, someone must enter the bag with the individual. Skin-to-skin contact is the most effective means of transferring body warmth and may save the person's life.

An old wives' tale about surviving the cold says shivering is good; it generates heat and will keep you alive. This is true to a certain extent, and the involuntary action of shivering is indeed generating heat, but it is also the first and possibly only recognizable symptom of hypothermia.

If you or any individual in your party begins to shiver, you should immediately become concerned about safety. As soon as someone is not comfortable, shivers, or complains about the cold, attention should be focused on warming the individual. It is important to remember that death from hypothermia is possible at outdoor temperatures up to 45 degrees F depending on the amount of wind and an individual's clothing.

WINDCHILL FACTOR
EQUIVALENT TEMPERATURES

WIND IN MILES PER HOUR

CURRENT TEMPERATURE (°F)	5	10	15	20	25	30	35	40	45	50
35	33	21	16	12	7	5	3	1	1	0
30	27	16	11	3	0	-2	-4	-4	-6	-7
25	21	9	1	-4	-7	-11	-13	-15	-17	-17
20	16	2	-6	-9	-15	-18	-20	-22	-24	-24
15	12	-2	-11	-17	-22	-26	-27	-29	-31	-31
10	7	-2	-18	-24	-29	-33	-35	-36	-38	-38
5	1	-15	-25	-32	-37	-41	-43	-45	-46	-47
0	-6	-22	-33	-40	-45	-49	-52	-54	-54	-56
-5	-11	-27	-40	-46	-52	-56	-60	-62	-63	-63
-10	-15	-31	-45	-52	-58	-63	-67	-69	-70	-70
-15	-20	-38	-51	-60	-67	-70	-72	-76	-78	-79
-20	-26	-45	-60	-68	-75	-78	-83	-87	-87	-88
-25	-31	-52	-65	-76	-83	-87	-90	-94	-94	-96
-30	-35	-58	-70	-81	-89	-94	-98	-101	-101	-103
-35	-41	-64	-78	-88	-96	-101	-105	-107	-108	-110
-40	-47	-70	-85	-96	-104	-109	-113	-116	-118	-120
-45	-54	-77	-90	-103	-112	-117	-123	-128	-128	-128

Extreme danger at windchill factor under –25°

WINDCHILL CHART

FROSTBITE

Frostbite of the extremities can occur in severe
cold. It is unmistakable, especially to the person
afflicted. The pain of cold in the extremity will
gradually subside until it becomes completely
numb and without sensation. The skin on the area
will be pale, and the extremity will feel hard like a
piece of wood.

Cover and protect the frostbitten area from
further cold damage until it can be thawed. Do not
rub the extremity to restore circulation or place it
in cold water or snow. Attempts to thaw frozen
extremities where there is a possibility they may
freeze again can cause more damage.

When you reach permanent shelter, the
extremity can be thawed in water between 98 and
104 degrees F. Within 20 minutes to an hour
circulation should be restored. During this period
there may be pain as the extremity warms.

Do not hold the extremity near an oven or open
flame. When all sensation is gone, it will be easy to
burn the frozen tissue.

Seek medical help as soon as possible.

POISONOUS BITES

Inexperienced outdoorsmen and people new to
areas inhabited by poisonous animals are often
unduly concerned about the danger from poisonous bites. Vehicle accidents caused by operator
carelessness and exposure to the elements present
a more significant threat to off-roaders than any
animal found in North America.

SNAKEBITE

Nearly 50,000 Americans are bitten by snakes each
year. Of these reported cases, only about 20
percent, or fewer than 10,000, involve poisonous
snakes and only a handful are fatal.

Mortality from snakebite is low, but the injury should always be treated as serious. If you are more than four hours from medical assistance, the danger from snakebite increases substantially.

There are only two North American snakes that are particularly dangerous: the eastern and western diamondback rattlesnakes. Fortunately, they prefer isolated areas and are equipped with a built-in alarm system.

Although its venom is deadly, the Arizona and eastern coral snakes are rare, shy, and equipped with a poor venom-delivery system. The coral snake has short fangs and a small mouth, making it difficult for its bite to penetrate clothing. The coral snake must hang onto its prey and "chew" the venom into a shallow wound.

Other poisonous North American snakes such as the cottonmouth (or water moccasin) and copperhead are frequent attackers in some states but rarely cause death or serious, lasting effects.

It is important to identify the snake when an individual is bitten. This will help determine the level of danger and proper medical care. If you are not sure about the snake species, kill it and take it with you to the hospital. Doctors will use the snake to help identify a proper antivenin. Snakes do not cover much ground. It will probably be within 40 feet of the attack location.

Obviously, if the snake has a rattle there is immediate reason for concern. If the snake does not have a rattle, inspection of the bite pattern may determine if the snake is poisonous. A poisonous snakebite will leave detectable fang punctures at either end of the teeth marks, depending on the angle of attack.

A snake replaces venom slowly after each feeding. Even if fang marks are noticeable, a significant percentage of all poisonous snakebites are delivered without enough venom to cause serious symptoms. As many as one in five bites are "dry" and will cause only mild to moderate symptoms.

At first glance the bright red, black, and yellow colors of a coral snake may be confused with the harmless scarlet king snake (southeastern race), scarlet snake, and western shovel-nosed snake. Unlike other snakes with red and black markings, the wide bands on coral snakes always extend completely around its body, and its head is black. The color sequence on coral snakes places yellow next to the red bands.

There is an old poem to help identify the poisonous coral snake. "Yellow head, red on black, friend of Jack; black head, red on yellow, deadly fellow."

When snakebite occurs, it is important to keep the victim quiet and warm. Have the victim lie down immediately with the bitten limb below the heart. Unnecessary movement will make the venom spread, worsening the symptoms. Reassure the patient that snakebites are almost never fatal.

If the bite is poisonous, symptoms will begin almost immediately. Typical first symptoms include mild swelling and moderate pain around the bite, tingling sensations, rapid pulse, poor vision, shortness of breath, weakness, nausea, and vomiting. The skin around the bite may change color.

Immediately after the victim is quieted, you may apply suction to the bite with a venom extractor. Snake venom is absorbed into tissue quickly. Unless the extractor is applied within 15 minutes after the strike, most of the venom will already be absorbed.

If you believe the bite is poisonous, you may apply a wide constricting band, **not a tourniquet**, 2 to 4 inches above the bite. The band should be at least 3/4 inch wide and just snug enough so you can slide your finger under it. **Never place the band on a joint or around the neck or torso.**

The band is applied to slow spreading of the venom through lymph vessels below the skin and should not stop circulation to the limb.

Circulation to the bitten limb must be verified periodically by feeling for pulse at the extremity. Be alert to swelling caused by the bite that may stop blood flow to the limb. Loosen the band as necessary to ensure a strong pulse in the limb, but do not remove it. A belt makes a suitable band if you do not have a snakebite kit.

Failure to ensure circulation may lead to permanent injury or even amputation of the limb.

Do not give the victim aspirin for pain. Aspirin can thin blood and worsen the effect of venom. A painkiller that does not include aspirin can be given to the victim.

Do not give the victim alcohol, sedatives, or other medications.

Cold compresses, ice packs, or sprays to chill the area of the bite are not recommended.

In severe snakebite cases, rapid swelling, numbness, and severe pain will develop quickly. The victim may go into shock or convulsions and experience twitching, slurred speech, or paralysis. If untreated, the victim's pulse and breathing will eventually stop.

Transport the victim to a hospital. If a medical facility can be reached within 4 or 5 hours, most victims should recover fully.

If the patient stops breathing or goes into full cardiac arrest, provide CPR to keep the victim alive until medical help can be reached. Most first-aid kits include step-by-step instructions for CPR.

Many doctors are fearful that snakebite first aid involving incisions might be worse than the bite.

After moving to Arizona, I asked my doctor about first aid for snakebite and was surprised at his response. He said he had treated scores of snakebite cases and found where the patient reached the hospital within 4 hours and first aid had been administered, more lasting damage was caused by improperly administered first aid than the snakebite.

I was puzzled by the doctor's comment until I met a fellow who insisted he nearly bled to death after being "snakebit." While trying to remove the venom, a friend cut a major artery in his lower leg with a large Bowie knife. I asked why the friend cut so deeply. The fellow insisted all they thought about was removing the poison. They reached a hospital within two hours— in time for a severe snakebite to be treated but almost too late for severe blood loss.

To be best informed, ask your doctor for professional advice regarding the removal of snake venom immediately after a bite.

AVOIDING SNAKEBITE

Even if you try to find one, you can spend days or weeks in snake-infested areas before happening onto a snake, and then chances are it will not even be poisonous. If you are still worried, consider that avoiding snakes and their bites is easy if you understand a few simple facts.

Much of a snake's movements are driven by its cold-blooded reptilian physiology. Since the snake cannot regulate its own metabolism, it has to be warmed or cooled by its environment and moves around accordingly.

In cool weather, the snake will sun itself in the open and may be found on a path, rock, or log. Unless it is coiled, it will not be able to strike. And even if coiled, a large snake will always prefer to slink away rather than attack something as large as a human.

If you talk, whistle, or make noise while you walk, chances are the most you will ever see of a snake is its tail slithering away when you get near.

In hot weather, the snake will seek a cool, shaded spot next to or under a rock, log, or man-made object.

Especially in desert heat you should check for snakes before you reach, step, or crawl into the shade. After you have been parked, the cool ground under your vehicle may be a perfect place for an overheated snake to cool off.

INSECT STINGS

While most people are concerned about poisonous spiders and scorpions, bees are actually far more dangerous and believed to kill more people each year than any other animal. Spider or scorpion bites may make an adult ill, but death or lasting effect is extremely rare.

Bees are dangerous for two reasons. Unlike other insects, bees congregate in large numbers. A victim can stumble into a large hive or swarm and receive a fatal number of stings. Many individuals, including the author of this book, get a fatal allergic reaction from even a single bee sting.

Everyone experiences slight burning, itching, minor swelling, and redness at the site of a sting. People with a more serious reaction may develop hives, headache, nausea, and severe swelling. Those who are endangered may experience swelling in the throat and difficulty breathing. Generally, the quicker the reaction, the more dangerous the condition.

People with the most severe reactions may exhibit few symptoms and simply slip into res-piratory and cardiac arrest within minutes. It is believed that each year a number of reported heart attack fatalities may be misdiagnosed bee sting reactions.

I had been stung dozens of times as a small child and never experienced a serious reaction until at about the age of 11 when I was stung on the lip by a yellow jacket. Within an hour, the side of my head had puffed out several inches, my eye had swollen shut, and I was feeling faint and having difficulty breathing. I will never forget the relief when a doctor injected epinephrine. It immediately opened my lungs, and within 15 minutes all swelling dis-appeared.

A few years later I was stung by a bee that flew in the window of a car in which I was riding. On this occasion there was no swelling. I simply grew pale, my breathing became shallow, and my pulse began to slow.

By the time I received help, my pulse had slowed to 60 beats per minute, and I was semiconscious.

There is only one sure treatment for severe bee sting reactions. An injection of adrenaline must be administered as quickly as possible. The victim should lie down to ensure circulation to the head while being rushed to emergency medical help.

For individuals who know they react severely to bee stings, but want to enjoy the outdoors, your doctor will prescribe a special kit. This prescription kit contains a syringe, antihistamine tablets, and epinephrine for self-administration of the curing drugs. This kit may also be effective for treatment of other poisonous insect bites. For more information, consult your physician.

For normal, minor symptoms there is a product that may be a welcome addition to your first-aid supplies. The Sawyer Extraction Pump is claimed to be the only kit proved by scientific studies to remove bee-sting poison. When using this kit, Sawyer recommends you do not remove the stinger until after the pump has been applied. The stinger provides a pathway for the poison to exit through the skin. The pump must be applied almost immediately to be effective.

People who have used the Sawyer Extraction Pump™ for treating normal symptoms claim it is more effective at eliminating pain and swelling than other remedies.

Victims of stings should always resist the instinct to rub the painful area until after it has been treated. There is often a venom sac containing more poison attached to the stinger. A hard rub will only inject the remaining poison. Care should be taken when removing the stinger for the same reason.

Ice or a small amount of meat tenderizer rubbed on the skin will help reduce swelling.

AVOIDING BEE STINGS
When people learn of my bee sting allergy, they are amazed how casual I am about it. I will sit quietly and let a bee land on me, check me out, and fly away.

I explain that bees sting instinctively to protect their hive. If you do not swat, run, or jump to threaten them, chances are they will realize you are not a flower and move on.

I am more afraid of people who act violently around bees. The screaming, jumping, swatting "beephobiac" is enough to make any creature frightened. Once bees are threatened, they may sting anyone in the area.

I also avoid bee stings by being careful where I step. An aggressive and dangerous North American wasp, the yellow jacket, hives in the ground and will attack anything that steps into its nest.

I have learned to be cautious around overgrown areas with loose, dry grass or decomposing wood. You can often hear the hive as you approach. The sound is distinctively different from above-ground hives. Bees in underground hives slap their wings on the dry grass, creating a higher-pitched "hiss" rather than the normal "buzz." If you hear this sound, go around. A step in the wrong place can get you several hundred stings and possibly a quick death.

11

Survival

EVALUATING YOUR SITUATION

If your vehicle will not operate safely, you will be forced to evaluate the seriousness of the situation and determine the best course of action for yourself and your passengers.

Remember that someone will be looking for you when you are long overdue at home. Please be patient. The authorities receive a lot of calls about people who are simply delayed a few hours. The authorities may wait one whole day after your party has been reported overdue before they launch a major search. If the weather is threatening, the search may be postponed until it clears.

Unless you know assistance is nearby or a member of your party needs immediate medical attention, it is safest to stay with the vehicle until you are rescued. The vehicle provides shelter, and when you raise the hood it is a highly visible sign that you are in trouble.

Extreme heat is the only weather condition that should drive you from your vehicle. Desert heat can be life-threatening if you are without enough water. If someone in your party is aged, in poor health, or not used to the weather, these conditions are even more dangerous. In desert heat, a healthy acclimated adult may require a gallon of water each day to stay alive. Individuals who are not used to the heat may suffer from heat exhaustion, even if plenty of fluids are available.

Try to recall the number of other vehicles you have seen in the vicinity, what time of day you saw them, and which direction they were going. Consult a map of the area. It will help you evaluate the odds of someone passing your location. Forest Service personnel rarely leave well-graded roads connecting campsites or ranger stations without a reason, so if you are truly off the beaten path, you cannot depend on a "green truck" happening by.

Sunday evening is the worst time to break down off road. Traffic tends to move into a remote area at the beginning of the weekend and then back out the same way Sunday afternoon. If you have ever camped through an entire week, you know it is possible to spend Monday through Friday without seeing another person. It seems as if Friday afternoon everyone stampedes to the wilderness, only to leave by Sunday. Most people will also avoid extremely rough roads late in the day near nightfall.

For the purpose of safety (and to get the most desirable camping spots), I generally try to be the first vehicle into an area and break camp before other campers so I will have traffic behind me when I leave.

Attracting Help

Always keep the hood up as a sign of breakdown. Stake out the appropriate distress signal using bright-colored trash bags. If you are surrounded by mountains with trails at higher elevations, these signals may be visible to other off-roaders as well as to a search airplane.

Try your CB radio if you have one. If you are fortunate enough to stall on high ground within a signal shot of another off-roader, a CB will reach help. The final chapter details a true experience when a CB provided a friend and me with medical assistance.

On numerous occasions when deep within mountain ranges I have not been able to reach anyone on my CB. If you do not reach someone on the first try, keep trying every 15 minutes.

CBs seem to be great for talking to truckers on an interstate highway somewhere across the continent late at night, but are not reliable in off-road emergency situations. Cellular telephones only work within a few miles of close-range transponders that are located in populated areas.

Single-side-band (SSB) VHF radios use a more reliable frequency that is almost certain of reaching help. SSB/VHF radios are used by ham operators and are capable of worldwide communication. The cost of mobile VHF transceivers has dropped significantly in recent years to under $300. Many areas of the country now have mountaintop VHF transponders that will boost the signal from these mobile units and allow direct connection with the AT&T telephone system. In theory, if you live in one of these areas, you can access the 911 emergency line or call the auto club. Unfortunately, mobile VHF frequencies are regulated by the Federal Communications Commission (FCC), and you will be required to pass a test for a legal voice-operator's license.

Watch for dust from other vehicles. Flash a mirror toward the dust cloud to attract attention.

If you become desperate, you may attract help by building a smoke signal with oil-soaked rags or green leaves and branches. Oily rags will make a black smoke visible against gray overcast skies, and green leaves or branches will produce a white smoke visible against a clear blue sky.

Whatever you do, be careful. Do not start a real forest fire to attract attention. You will be required to pay for all costs associated with fighting the fire when you are rescued.

PICKING YOUR ROUTE

If you must leave your vehicle, do not simply head off toward a spot on the map. You should be careful and consider all the factors. Foot trails, ranches, cabins, and service facilities will be clearly marked on maps, but the route may be difficult or there may be other, closer places to find help.

Campsites are a good place to seek help. Campsites will probably be occupied on weekends, and they are frequented by Forest Service personnel who collect fees and make sure fires are out when everyone else has left. Much of the public land in the West is used for grazing by ranchers who maintain line shacks along fence boundaries.

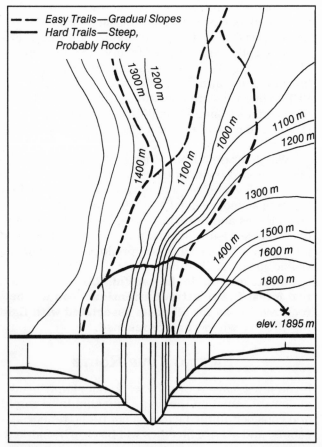

TOPOGRAPHICAL MAP CONTOURS

The line shacks may be labeled as "building" or "structure" and are often located near a line on the map which indicates the fence. The line shack should provide food, water, and shelter. Remember the code of the West. Go back later to replace anything you remove from these shacks so others in need can find provisions.

When you have identified places on the map where you might find help, review the surrounding topography. Unlike other maps, a topographical map has altitude contour lines that can be used to determine how difficult a trail will be to travel. Trails that parallel contour lines are flat and will be easy to travel. Routes that cross contour lines are on a grade. The closer the crossed contour lines, the steeper the grade. From the elevation label on each contour line you can determine which direction of travel is up- or downhill. This information is extremely important if you plan to walk the route. You can walk two or three times faster downhill. Depending on area terrain, it may be better to select a destination that is a little farther away but all downhill.

Try to follow a vehicle trail so you can be spotted by ground rescuers or wave down a passing off-roader. Foot trails are much harder to travel and will make you consume more energy and water than easy vehicle trails.

Do not be tempted to take a shortcut across a desert flat. There are several reasons why this is not a good idea, even if it looks safe and easy. First, the route probably has natural obstructions. Otherwise, the road would not go around the area. You can expect large washes or a lot of loose sand, and either will sap your energy.

Second, distances are deceptive in the desert. What appears to be a couple miles is often much farther, and it is easy to become disoriented in the sameness of a large desert flat.

Finally, if you leave the road, the odds of being spotted by rescuers are reduced. If you see a vehicle coming, you may not reach the road in time to stop it.

Unless you know the area or are a skilled outdoorsman, you should stay on the largest trail you can find.

GOING FOR HELP

If you decide to venture for help, make sure you leave the hood up and a note on the windshield

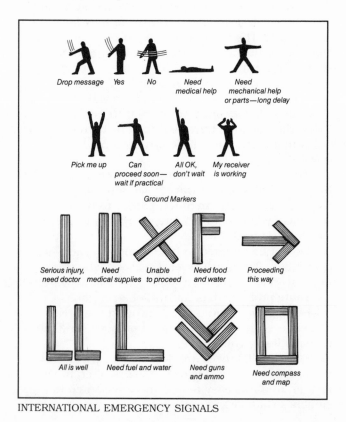

INTERNATIONAL EMERGENCY SIGNALS

describing your direction of travel and planned destination. You should place the appropriate ground marker(s) even if you are not yet overdue on the off chance a plane will spot your distress signal. Do not split your party if everyone is healthy and in reasonably good condition.

Take appropriate survival items with you. If in the desert, you should carry as much water as possible, salt tablets, extra clothing, and a blanket or sheet of plastic for shade from the sun. Take a salt tablet regularly to help prevent heat exhaustion or sunstroke.

Wear your clothing loosely, but remain fully clothed with the head covered. Walk at a slow conservative pace to avoid heat exhaustion. Stop and rest frequently. I always carry an inexpensive reflective survival blanket while hiking in the desert. It provides cool shade and is great to nap under in 110 degree heat.

In cold weather, you will only need a canteen of water, but you should carry high-calorie food and extra clothing. Candy bars or sweets are perfect for replenishing calories and help to prevent hypothermia. Avoid sweating by removing layers of clothing as you become warm, and cover with more clothing when cold. If you can, continue moving and avoid resting.

The survival-gear list will allow your party to travel quite a distance. You may be tempted to leave blankets or sleeping bags behind if it is hot, but this will be a big mistake if you are required to spend the night outside.

WATER

You will survive a long time without water if it is cool, but in extreme heat you will need large quantities of water to stay alive. At a cool 50 degrees F, an average adult can survive indefinitely on a quart of water daily or about 10 days with no water. At 120 degrees and 2.5 gallons of water per person, the survival time is still reduced to only two or three days.

You may find water anywhere if you know where to look. The wilderness is full of many signs. Animal trails usually lead downhill to water. Birds fly to water in the early morning and evening.

Water is most often located at the base of rock outcroppings, large hills and mountains, canyon heads, or low places on the terrain near green vegetation. Look for mineral stains on rocks from water dripping during the wet season or drying in rock potholes.

Your Forest Service map will show where water may be located, but odds are it will only be flowing

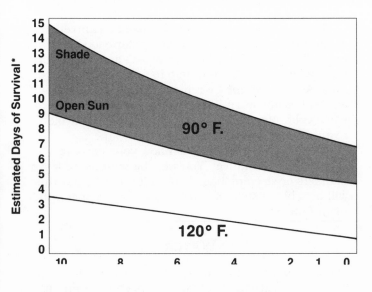

*No Walking in daytime heat—Walking at night only

DAYS OF SURVIVAL

during the wet season. If you find a promising place
that sustains green vegetation, there may be water
just below the surface. Dig a hole on the outside of
a dry river bend near the vegetation and wait at
least two hours to determine whether water is below
the surface.

Any water you find may not be safe to drink.
You should never drink stagnant water without first
disinfecting it. Never drink desert water that will
not support algae or green vegetation. It is poisoned
with alkali and will need to be distilled first.

There are several effective ways to disinfect bad
water. The safest is to disinfect the water with heat.
Boil the water for 20 minutes, let it stand for one-
half hour so any particles settle, and then strain it
before drinking. Boiling water with charcoal from a
fire will remove most bad tastes and odors.

Most people disinfect water chemically with
commercially manufactured purification tablets.
Not all commercial tablets will kill a particularly
tough protozoan called *Giardia lamblia* that is
common in dry areas. This bug causes what is
commonly called "hikers disease." It is washed into
standing water from animal feces in the form of a
dormant, shielded cyst. When you drink the water,
the cysts will quickly "hatch" and multiply in your
intestines. The resulting symptoms of diarrhea,
vomiting, weakness, and weight loss develop 7 to 14
days after the water is ingested. If you travel in the
desert, confirm the tablets you buy are effective
against *G. lamblia.*

Tincture of iodine from a first-aid kit or common
household bleach will disinfect stagnant water in
wet or temperate climates but will not kill *G. lamblia.* Add 1 drop of iodine or 2 drops of bleach to
each quart of water and shake vigorously. Allow the
water to stand for 30 minutes before you drink it.

The clear plastic sheet included on your list of
survival gear will make a solar still that is capable of

producing a quart of pure water every two to three hours in hot weather.

Locate an open spot near some vegetation. Ideally the spot will be on the outside of a dry river bend near large green vegetation. Dig a hole in the ground at least three feet deep. Place a container in the bottom of the hole and cover the hole with a single layer of plastic. The still will be more efficient and produce more water if the plastic is clear, but any nonpermeable material can be used. Seal the edges of the plastic around the hole with sand, and then place a rock in the middle of the sheet of plastic so it sags over the container.

The sun will heat moist sand in the hole causing it to condense on the underside of the plastic. The condensation will roll down the plastic to the rock and drip into the container. If the ground does not contain enough moisture to make the still work, you can place vegetation, urine, or radiator coolant in

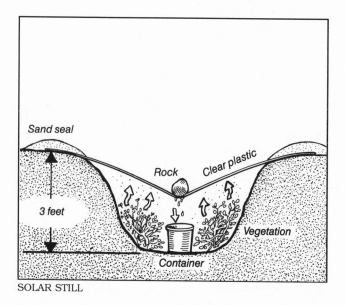

SOLAR STILL

the hole as a source of water. Line the bottom of
the hole with another piece of plastic or waterproof
material to prevent liquids you may add from soak-
ing into the dry sand. If possible, do not remove
the top plastic from the hole until several hours
after sundown. The still works best when the air
outside is cool and air in the hole is hot and humid.

The solar still can be used to remove sea salt,
alkali, or organisms from water that you know is
dangerous.

In extreme cold the need for water is greatly
reduced, but you will need to prevent heat loss
whenever possible. Both snow and ice are sources
of water, but ice is denser and takes less energy to
melt. If you have a choice, you should always eat
ice rather than snow because it uses less of your
body warmth. If you must, melt snow in your
hand before drinking it to conserve calories.

Desert temperatures fall below freezing nearly
every evening in the winter. Unfortunately, there is
often no more standing water in the winter than
during the heat of the summer. A solar still will
not produce much water in cold weather, so you
will need to find other sources of water.

The morning desert frost will provide water if
ice crystals are scraped off the rocks or vegetation.

If urine is frozen, the first crystals to form are
pure water and can be safely consumed.

Healthy birds, snakes, and other animals are a
safe source of valuable water if they can be caught.
Avoid eating any sick or injured animal you find.

SHELTER

At temperatures colder than 50 degrees F or
warmer than 95 degrees F, shelter is critical to
survival.

In cold weather your vehicle is the safest place

to wait for rescue. Temperature inside a vehicle will not drop below the outside ambient temperature and may get slightly higher due to captured body heat. The vehicle will provide excellent shelter from the wind. Even at survivable ambient temperatures, high wind can produce conditions that are extremely dangerous. A 30-mph wind at 35 degrees F will produce a below-zero windchill temperature. By huddling together inside a vehicle and using all available sources of insulation, you can survive indefinitely at 35 degrees, but you will only survive a few hours in the open at below-zero temperatures.

When the ambient temperature inside the vehicle falls below 45 degrees F, hypothermia may threaten

SNOW SHELTER

your life. If you choose to remain inside the vehicle
and run the engine for heat, make sure the exhaust
pipe is clear of obstructions and vented away from
the vehicle. Open a window slightly to help prevent
carbon monoxide poisoning. If you are caught in a
blizzard, keep the vehicle covered with snow for
added insulation. When the sun shines brightly,
you should remove snow from windows to allow the
warming sun to enter. If the vehicle is painted a
dark color, also remove snow from the roof so it will
absorb heat from the sun. Cover the vehicle with
snow again at night to reduce heat loss.

As soon as the snowstorm clears, use ground
markers as a distress signal. Do not clear snow
from around the vehicle unless you have no other
way to signal your presence.

If you become desperate for heat, you can build a
fire outside your vehicle. Position the fire on the
downwind side, just outside an open door. A tarp or
piece of plastic placed over the roof and top of the
door will direct much of the heat into the vehicle.
Allow an opening for smoke to exit. If you are
without dry fire fuel, siphon gasoline from the gas
tank. Pour the gas on wet fuel and allow it to soak
in. Carefully light the gas-soaked fuel away from the
vehicle. When the gasoline has flashed off and the
fire fuel begins to burn, move the fire closer to the
vehicle. Use gasoline sparingly and never pour it
directly on an open flame. Do not store unused
gasoline inside the vehicle. You may be overcome by
fumes and it is a major fire hazard.

If you do not want to stray from your vehicle but
the desert heat is extremely uncomfortable, crawl
underneath where it will be cooler. If it is a tight fit,
dig out some of the warmer surface sand. Do not
forget to set the emergency brake and block the
tires.

If the heat is still unbearable, you might be
forced to look for a cooler place to wait. Scan the

area for rock outcroppings. You may want to explore any overhang with a northerly exposure for
shelter from the heat. If you are lucky enough to
find a cave, the temperature inside may be 10 to 25
degrees cooler.

The following illustrations provide ideas for
makeshift desert shelters you can create in the open
from available material. The key to these shelters is
the hole dug below the hot surface sand. If you are
lucky, sand two or three feet below the surface will
be damp, creating a nice cooling effect as moisture
evaporates. Evaporation will be helped if you align
the openings to prevailing winds.

The windchill chart on page 119 is based on dry

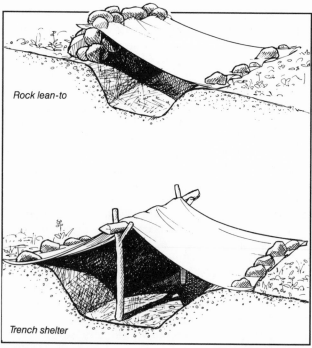

Rock lean-to

Trench shelter

DESERT SHELTERS

conditions. If you get wet, hypothermia can occur at temperatures above 45 degrees windchill. In rainy weather you should choose to remain safe and dry inside the vehicle until the storm blows over. Venturing outside could be fatal if the wind blows.

There is only one factor that might drive you from the vehicle in cold, wet weather. If you are on a flat or in a low spot, look on the branches of bushes and trees to determine how high the water level rises. I have seen desert flotsam stuck in the top of mesquite 20 feet off the ground. You will not want to wait out the storm in the middle of a flash-flood plain.

If you are worried about being caught in a flash flood and cannot move the vehicle, build a makeshift shelter anywhere above the high-water mark with a plastic sheet. A plastic sheet can be thrown across any large bush, tied between trees, or simply draped over your head for shelter. Your objective is to stay dry and out of the wind. Try to pick the top of a protected knoll or rise so water will drain away from the shelter.

CLOTHING

Proper clothing is important for survival in heat or cold.

There is a good reason why Arabs do not roam the Sahara in shorts. No matter how "burn-proof" you think your skin is, it will bake within hours if not covered from the desert sun.

Wear loose, light-colored clothing when you go to the desert. A wide-brimmed straw hat, loose white shirt, blue jeans or long shorts, and good hiking boots are perfect in the heat.

If you respect the unpredictability of the wilderness, you will always carry cold-weather clothing to the desert. I have seen the Sonoran Desert freeze at night in July, and the Mohave reach 100 degrees F in

January. Either temperature extreme will kill if you
are not prepared.

I recommend the following clothing for desert
heat and for cold protection down to freezing temperatures:

> Two pairs of socks with reinforced heel and toe
> Good hiking boots
> Insulated underwear or ski pants
> Wool or synthetic pants
> Long khaki shorts or blue jeans
> T-shirt
> Loose-fitting white long sleeve shirt
> Sweatshirt or sweater
> Stocking cap or thick, tight-fitting, cotton hat
> Straw hat or wide-brimmed hat
> Long, goose down jacket
> Gloves or mittens

It is important that you are able to stay dry. An
extra pair of dry socks will help. Wool or the new
loop-pile synthetic pants wick moisture away from
the skin and will keep you warmer than cotton blue
jeans.

Much of the body's heat loss is from the head. A
good, thick stocking cap can be pulled down over
your head and will cut heat loss substantially.

Anyone who has worked outside where the
weather gets extremely cold knows it is important to
wear several layers of clothing. Do not try to dress
for the cold with only one or two layers of garments.
To stay warm, **you must stay dry**; even the moisture from minor perspiration will make you more
susceptible to hypothermia. Multiple layers of
clothing allow you to add or remove a layer as
needed to stay comfortable. I have worn all the
following clothing while working or ice-fishing in
subzero weather. Even this amount of clothing will

not guarantee survival in subzero weather for more than a few hours without shelter from the wind.

Thermoknit undershirt (long sleeve)
Flannel shirt (double thick)
Sweatshirt or sweater
Thermoknit underpants
Blue jeans
One-piece snowsuit
Down-filled, long, arctic parka with hood
Knit head cover with hole for eyes and mouth
Thick, knit stocking cap
Rabbit fur-lined leather gloves
Insulated mittens
Two pairs of wool socks
Felt-lined Sorel boots

There are many new lightweight synthetics that have superior warming and water-shedding properties. While this clothing is expensive it is also durable and will last for many years. If you want safety, comfort, and the convenience of light weight, go to a good expedition outfitter's store and inquire about clothing. The staff will show you the latest clothing and explain the merits of the new materials.

In addition to proper wilderness attire, you should never venture off road without sleeping bag(s) rated to at least 30 degrees F. If you travel with several people, you will want at least one bag for every two individuals. A mummy bag can snugly fit two people. If you are short of bags, someone might be left in the cold to die.

12

The Environment

Most people recognize our obligation to conserve nature, but public debate over how to do it often pits off-roaders and environmental groups against each other.

Environmentalists would like to close national forests to ORVs. Off-roaders argue that vehicles do not cause permanent damage or that the damage is not justification for closures. We, obviously, do not want to lose our chosen recreation, but denial of the problem will save neither the environment nor off-roading.

Off-roaders who are honest about what they have seen must admit that ORVs can damage the environment, especially when driven by selfish, unconcerned individuals. Unfortunately, there are enough "bad apples" to ruin it for everyone.

Like other environmentalists, I have seen beautiful mountain meadows cut from end to end by 3-foot 4 X 4 trenches or motorcycle "whoop-de-dos" 6 feet high and 20 feet wide. One particularly beautiful meadow I know that was "plowed up" four years ago is eroding away a little each year. The jerk that first drove his rig through the meadow started a chain of events that will only end with the total loss of this spot. Even desert wagon tracks that have not been traveled for 100 years are still visible.

Americans have only been environmentally aware for the past two decades. Much of the worst desert scarring occurred before 1970 when there was little effort to manage arid lands and people were insensitive to the environment. Thanks to better land management and increased public awareness, abuses have nearly stopped in many areas, but the old scarring will remain for generations.

Pressure on the wilderness from expanding population has never been so great. Damage from

ORVs is leading to the closure of public lands at a rapid rate. Millions of acres that had been open to mechanized transportation have been closed, and now you must walk or ride a horse to see areas off the maintained roads. If you ride a dirt motorcycle, you are particularly sensitive to the impact the Wilderness Act has had. Many of the best dirt-bike trails are now closed as part of legislation to protect the environment.

Even if you never abuse the wilderness, there are enough who do to make all off-roaders "the bad guys." To protect the environment and your right to use an ORV, you must follow the rules and encourage the education of others.

Do not tolerate abusers. If you witness an off-roader doing something wrong, attempt to explain the repercussions of his actions. I believe most people inflict harm on the environment out of ignorance and selfishness. We cannot do anything about selfishness, but a lecture or some verbal abuse may help educate.

Always stay on approved routes. You should have a map provided by the Forest Service, Park Service, or Bureau of Land Management that shows the approved off-road trails. Not only will this map keep you out of trouble with the authorities, it also allows the authorities to control damage with temporary closures to keep the area open for your future use. Public lands need to be managed. Temporary closures give the environment a chance to rejuvenate so it can be opened again in the future. If you break this rule, you will surely be contributing to the eventual permanent closure of the area.

Only rocky streambeds can continue to receive traffic without damage. If you want to drive to a meadow or along smooth, tree-lined trails, understand that these types of trails are more sensitive to

ORV damage and must be periodically closed.

You can help keep your favorite areas open. If you see a bad rut in the trail, stop and fill it with rocks and dirt to help stop erosion. If you belong to an off-road club, encourage participation in the Forest Service Adopt-a-Trail program to help maintain your favorite trail.

Try to block all new unauthorized trails with rocks or logs. It is amazing how one idiot's set of tracks seems to be an open invitation for every other "destroyer" to follow. I know several places where someone tried to climb a hill and now the whole side of the mountain has been clawed away and is eroding because of idiots that thought it was OK to follow the tracks. What had been a beautiful valley now looks like a gravel pit.

Write down the license plate number of any violator for the authorities and scold anyone stuck where the driver should not have gone. I will no longer pull a vehicle out of a hole if its operator was obviously testing the rig off the main trail. This person deserves all the expense or inconvenience he gets and only deserves a lift to the local Forest Service office.

Never camp at an isolated water hole. If you want to camp near water, find a lake or stream. Your presence near an isolated water hole will disrupt animal habitat and may even drive wildlife from the area. I knew an isolated spring in Joshua Tree National Monument that was used every evening by the rare desert bighorn sheep. A hike of only a few hours off a graded road afforded an opportunity to see these magnificent creatures. One summer I witnessed a party of hikers camping at the spring. No one has seen the sheep at this spot since. This one ignorant action may have made it impossible for most people to enjoy these animals. Ironically, the campers probably never saw the sheep or even knew of their existence.

Do not dig trenches, latrine holes, or fire pits.
You should never dig large holes at a campsite.
When you leave, it should look just like when you
first arrived. Most people pick the same area to
camp. If everyone dug a latrine hole, new fire pit,
and a trench around his or her tent, the campsite
would quickly be reduced to rocks and gravel from
erosion. Twenty years ago, the Boy Scout Handbook
instructed campers to do this, but today there is too
much pressure on the wilderness for this practice to
continue.

Desert areas are extremely sensitive to human
presence. By definition, the desert is without regular rain to help to decompose human waste and
wash away your scent. Human excrement should
not be buried in one place, and members of your
party should be instructed to avoid defecating near
animal trails. Urinating on an animal trail can stop
use of the trail for days or weeks. Dig "cat holes"
three to six inches deep and bury excrement. If
possible, pack out all used toilet paper or burn it
before it is buried. Appreciate that animals are
fearful of man throughout the lower 48 states and
know his scent well. If you want to see wildlife, then
avoid driving them away from popular camping
spots.

Carry all your trash out. Most people are good
about not leaving trash behind, but because of
"slackers" we should also pick up other people's
trash without hesitation. Carry the trash out of the
area to be discarded in a proper place. Do not bury
trash at campsites.

Do not be a noise polluter. Some people seem to be
attracted to wilderness areas so they can "let it all
out" without upsetting civilization. To these people

the outdoors is synonymous with partying, yelling, hot-rodding, and noise. Others seem to be so addicted to the noises of civilization they bring it along in the form of loud stereos which are used to cover up the quiet and serenity for which most people are searching.

I find it nearly impossible to cope with individuals who cannot enjoy quiet and must fill the outdoors with loud music. I am normally a peaceful individual, but have been know to threaten people over music played so loudly everyone within three miles had to listen.

Most campgrounds have rules that prohibit excessive noise. Unfortunately, there are not enough rangers to prevent abuses. If you like to play music in campgrounds, understand that unlike the city, in a quiet campground it will carry long distances and seem louder because there is no background noise to cover it up.

Next on my list of "noise polluters to hate" is dirt bikers who do not know when to back off the throttle. I own three dirt bikes and know how hard it is to keep a motocross bike quiet, but you are being rude if you fail to recognize the amount of noise you make. If everyone slows down around camps or hikers, we may have a place to ride again next year.

Motorcyclists should be sensitive to potential damage. My favorite form of wilderness transportation is a dirt bike. I prefer to ride remote hiking trails, 30 or 50 miles in from the nearest gravel roads. If you are a dirt biker, you have noticed there have been more closures affecting motorcycles than any other ORV.

Unfortunately, the modern dirt bike poses the biggest threat to remote areas. Dirt bikes can travel in areas 4-wheel vehicles cannot, making them difficult for authorities to control. And perhaps the most troubling attributes of the modern dirt bikes are aggressive tire tread and tremendous power.

I mentioned "whoop-de-dos" earlier. There seems to be no limit to how high, long, or wide these big bumps can get. The largest I have seen were over my head, about one half mile long and 100 yards wide.

I have studied deteriorating motorcycle trails by observing bikers drive through. The damage first occurs at the beginning of an open flat with good visibility, at the base or top of hills, or at the end of a curve. A typical motorcyclist entering these areas opens the throttle and spins the rear knobby tire. The aggressive tread will dig up anything under three inches in diameter.

"Whoop-de-dos" are created at the beginning of an opening into a flat where everyone goes to full power. When the first big hole is dug, everyone cracks the throttle immediately beyond and starts another one, on and on down the trail. Then the hotdoggers who like to get airborne use them as jumps and dig them even deeper. Once they are deep enough to be a real pain to the rest of us, we drive alongside, and the bumps begin to grow laterally.

What I have also noticed is motorcycles of a particular design seem to have more impact on trails. Motocross bikes only have one function: to go fast. They were designed for motocross tracks, not narrow trails, and contrast with the once popular enduro. Until the mid-1970s, many dirt bikes were designed with a smooth usable power band and slow-speed controllability.

A modern motocross bike, the antithesis of the early enduro, is anything but controllable to the average rider. The raw snappy power and high top end of the motocross bike may attract trendy young buyers who want to be hotdogs, but unfortunately, the bike also does a lot of damage, resulting in closure of your favorite trails.

I believe some motorcycle designs may do less trail damage than horses and are nearly as quiet. Examples include trials bikes (designed for observed trials or enduro competition) that have less power, heavy flywheels, nonaggressive tire tread, and good mufflers. My favorite motorcycle is an old Bultaco Alpina enduro/trials bike. It is so quiet I can sneak up on hikers before they know I am there, and it has a smooth controllable power band that rarely digs a rut. The old "taco" 360-cc displacement engine provides more than enough raw torque for any riding condition under 45 mph.

If you like to ride a wide range of motorcycle trails and particularly enjoy putting through the trees or along streams, you may want to stay away from the newer, trendy, large-displacement, water-cooled, two-stroke motocross bikes and buy a good light, dual-purpose four-stroker. You will find they are easier to ride and less disruptive to the environment. You may even find that in extremely rough terrain you will leave the motocross hotdogs far behind.

13

A True Experience

This unfortunate and embarrassing incident is being shared with you as an example of poor judgment that can cause a life-threatening situation. Like most people, I thought these things always happened to the other guy.

I had not seen my friend Fred for six months. I heard that he was building a 4X4 in a garage just down the freeway from where I lived in Orange County, California.

One Sunday morning in January, he arrived in my driveway with his project: a 1956 4-wheel-drive Willys panel truck, painted county-truck yellow, with huge tires, and powered by a rebuilt International six-cylinder motor. The interior was not finished, and there were miscellaneous spare parts, plywood, and tools in the back. The engine, the biggest six-banger ever built, looked as long as an antique straight-eight.

We drove around the block with Fred showing me how low the "Yellow Beast" was geared. He did not replace the original gearbox and driveline, and the thing would cr-a-a-w-w-l down the street with the engine spinning at at least 4,000 rpms.

I had to see what the Yellow Beast would do off pavement. After some coaxing (no more than one and a half appeals and my willingness to pay for the gas), we were on our way up Ortega Highway to the crest of Cleveland National Forest for a good test run.

It was a typical dreary January morning along the coast with low early morning clouds. As we ascended the mountains heading north, the sun began to shine, and the weather seemed to clear.

Near the top of the highway, our first problem developed. I smelled something burning. Fred replied, "Must be the new paint on the exhaust." Then I turned around and saw electrical arcing. I yelled, and we pulled over to the side of the road.

Fred had relocated the battery in a wooden box behind the passenger seat. The hot terminal of the battery had touched the side of the body. "Juice" from the new alternator and the huge, deep-draw, marine battery welded the terminal to the side of the body. We disconnected the negative cable and pried the battery away from metal. (The paint on Fred's Willys now had a nice black spot weld about 2 inches in diameter through to the outside immediately behind the passenger seat.)

There was not much conversation from Fred. He just muttered about the paint for a while.

At the crest of the range we turned west toward Santiago Peak on the road that would eventually lead to Silverado Canyon and home. We were proud of having picked such a perfect test loop

OVER THE EDGE

with no major obstacles but some traffic in case we developed any serious mechanical failures.

The morning turned out to be a blast. Recent rain had filled normally dry washes so we could "pan for color" in a couple of places.

It was about 1:00 P.M. and we were only 20 miles from paved roads back to suburbia. There was no reason to worry about time. The ranger on duty in the Santiago lookout tower was apparently bored or lonely (not much chance of a fire that day) and allowed us to climb the long ladder to the top of his tower.

From the 5,500-foot lookout the panoramic view was spectacular. Toward the ocean, over the 6 million people of Orange County, you could see every landmark with exceptional clarity. The islands off the coast and most of the basin were brightly sunlit with only an occasional cloud shadowing the foot-hills. Behind us toward the San Bernardino Mountains, dark ominous clouds extended overhead toward the ocean.

It was as if our backs were against a dark wall and our heads under a low ceiling. We looked out across a city unaware of weather moving into the Los Angeles area. It may have been the sunshine and sense of well-being at home that made us unconcerned about weather conditions just to the north.

We left the tower and continued down the road. It was not long before the clouds from the north descended, creating mist. It would remain light for several more hours and it was not raining; so we were not concerned.

Several bends farther down the road from the top of Santiago Peak we came upon a pickup truck, carrying three cowboys, which had managed to slide off the road into a ditch.

It was obvious they had been drinking and driving too fast, but we gave the driver a lift back up Santiago where he had friends waiting.

It was now about 3:30. The clouds were getting thicker, darker, and wetter. The misting had changed to a slow drizzle. We were still only 15 miles from Silverado Canyon, normally only a short, hour drive on this road.

Then it happened. Fred came into a corner and applied the brakes, and the pedal went to the floor. Fortunately, the Yellow Beast was geared so low that the engine quickly brought us to a stop.

"Yep," Fred said looking under the front, "The left front cylinder is leaking. I knew I should have fixed that." I replied, "Let's just top off the reservoir and bleed the brakes. Got any fluid?"

After rummaging around in the Beast, a few expletives, and shouting over a lack of brake fluid, we decided it would be safe to continue in "granny" gear and the low 4-wheel-drive gear range.

In this gear the Willys would not go over 5 mph when floored and quickly stopped *if* the gas pedal was lifted.

It was now 4:00 and getting dark. There was a fog developing as the temperature allowed the cloud cover to descend even further down the mountain. We were making slow positive headway, but so was the fog cover. By 4:30, the fog was so thick we could not see the mountain beside us.

The lights on top of the cab were useless and only served to blind us. The stock low beams alone helped us to see the road ahead. Visibility progressively worsened until Fred was watching the ground out his side of the truck and I was watching on my side. Other than the blinding light reflected back from the fog in front, there was total darkness around us.

We were both nervous. We had driven this road many times and knew the edge fell off a thousand feet all along this side of the mountain.

"Can you see the road on your side? I can't see anything over here."

"We're all right. I can see where they have graded and piled up dirt," I replied.

And so it went for another few miles. Then I felt the left front wheel crawl off the edge. I yelled, "We're going over!"

Fred did not say a thing and tried to keep the vehicle upright. The Beast was committed to a course over the edge as if it was following the white lights reflecting from the fog. I grabbed the door handle and jerked to get it open. The door would not open. I tried again and pushed with my shoulder as the Beast rolled toward Fred's side.

Everything seemed to shift into slow motion as the door finally opened and I flopped out. Gravity closed the door and dragged it across my legs, as the Beast, now on its side, rolled one way and I the other. I remember seeing the underbody of the truck as I fell to the ground alongside. We each tumbled through the air.

Then I heard the sound of metal crunching on impact with the mountain: boom . . . bang, boom-boom, crash (long pause), boom. I thought the horrible sound would stop at any time, but it went on and on down the mountain, cracking off brush and trees as the Beast's body rotated around the engine in midair only to impact again, getting fainter and fainter until it came to rest somewhere down in the dark.

Finally, silence. Time returned to normal. I lay on my back thinking, while the drizzle drifted lightly onto my face. "With a sound like that, Fred has to be dead," I thought. "There is no way he could have survived."

I called out anyway, "Fred! Hey, Fred!" I did not want him to answer. I did not want him to be suffering. I hoped it was over quickly. I knew my arm was broken from the fall. I had never broken an arm before, but I thought, "This must be what it feels like."

"I've got to get back to the road," I thought. "It's dark and raining. What if no one is still up here? I'll have to walk to get help."

I looked around but saw only darkness. There was not enough light to see the ground next to my head. I tried to climb the side of the steep hill with my arm clutched to my stomach. The tennis shoes I wore slipped on loose gravel, and I cartwheeled back down the mountain slope coming to rest lower than where I had been before.

I do not know how long I was unconscious. When I regained consciousness, it seemed later, wetter, colder, darker, and lonelier.

I knew I was in poor shape to make it to the road. I was now wet to the bone. I was shaking, and my arm hurt. I felt nauseous and wanted to vomit, but the thought of hurting my arm even more stopped me.

I concentrated on the shaking. When I could not get it to stop, I felt better. I knew if I continued to shake I was not near death from hypothermia. I began to take a perverse comfort in pain from the broken arm. If it hurt, I was conscious and not in shock.

Then, I thought, "Maybe its easier to go *down* the mountain from here. I wonder if Fred managed to get out down there."

I yelled again toward nowhere, "Fred! Hey, Fred!"

From down in the darkness came a low-pitched "Uhhh."

"Hey, Fred! You all right?" I shouted.

In a low, slow voice from below, "I'm all right, I'm all right." Then louder, "No...! I can't see! I can't see!" Then softer again, "It's just blood in my eyes."

"Oh, no," I thought to myself. "He's not dead. Now I've got to go down there to try to help him, too."

I did not want to be a hero—just alive. I knew
my life was threatened, and instincts of self preservation were taking over.

I had to get out. But how?

Then I heard footsteps on the gravel down below.
Crunch...crunch, then crunch-crunch, and running.

Before I knew it, Fred was nearby. He was
pulling on my broken arm and babbling nonsense
as I cried out in pain. Fred screeched hysterically,
"We've got to get out! Now! Hurry! Come on!"

Overhead I could see headlights reflecting in the
fog as a truck came around a corner.

We both clutched rocks to throw up over our
heads. When the truck sounded as if it was directly
over us, we let go.

"What the hell!" came from above. "Someone's
throwing rocks at us!"

"Ssshhh!" from another voice. "Listen. Someone's calling help."

"Heeeeelp! Heeeeelp!"

Fred suddenly ran like a mountain goat to the
top of the road. I could hear his fast shrill voice.
"Me and my buddy were driving along and the front
wheel went over the edge, and . . . and he's still
down there." And then he went stiff and out like a
light, with a "face plant" in the dirt. Fred woke up
sometime the next day.

I rode down the mountain in the bed of the
truck, pain at every bump. Fred moaned a lot and
was in shock, so the good Samaritans thought he
belonged near the heater. Probably so.

Their truck had a CB that they used to call the
highway patrol. It was a straight shot to civilization
from the side of Saddleback. Paramedics were
waiting for us at the base of the dirt road.

Fred only broke one bone, his nose, which now
points west when he looks north. He received cuts
and bruises, but otherwise was OK.

My arm was badly broken, and I suffered for

some time without a cast because there was not
enough bone in one piece for the doctors to set. But
after about a year, it was as good as new with full
mobility and no worse for the wear.

There was not much left of the Yellow Beast.
When it first rolled over on its side, the spot rivets
around the top gave way. When it began to rotate
around the engine, bouncing on its ends, the frame
buckled and the top popped loose.

Fred says the last thing he remembers after
rolling sideways a few times is the headlights shin-
ing directly into the dirt as he held on for dear life,
like Slim Pickens in the movie *Dr. Strangelove*,
rodeo riding to the end.

On impact he broke the steering wheel with his
head and bounced around inside the Beast for a
while until it coughed him out through the top and
laid him down in a six-foot-round patch of soft
sand. THE ONLY SANDY SPOT in the area.

The Beast continued down the mountain like a
manufactured Hollywood movie stunt throwing off
pieces on the way—first the top, then the doors,
hood, cowling, and interior—until the frame and
pan with engine and driveline came to rest upside
down.

Officials said we were the only two people ever to
have driven off that corner (called appropriately
Dead Man's Curve) and lived.

Our survival was pure luck. We should not
have allowed ourselves to get into the situation that
caused the accident. I hope everyone who reads
this true account can learn from our experience.

We broke every rule of common sense:

- Do not drive without brakes
  or if the vehicle is not safe.
- Do not drive when you have poor
  visibility and cannot see the road.

- Carry spare parts and supplies.
- Ignore agendas if they are at the expense of safety.
- Pay attention to weather conditions.
- Check out your vehicle before you venture off road.

Index

Accessories, 70, 108
Adopt-a-Trail program, 148
Air compressor, 112
Alternator, 65; failure, 65; fuses, 67; testing, 68
Alternator/regulator designs, 67
Ammeter, 65
Antifreeze, 72
Astro Turf, 108-9
Automatic transmission: adjusting linkage, 99-100; fluid, 85;
    using motor oil in, 99; slippage, 97-98
Auxiliary lights, 108

Battery, 65; cable connections, 52; conserving charge,19;
    dead, 53; extending life of, 69; low charge, 53; recharging, 33,
    69; short, 69; testing, 52
Bearings, bad, 101
Bee stings, 125-28; avoiding, 127-28; symptoms, 125;
    treatment, 126-27. *See also* Yellow jacket
Brakes, 104; adjusting shoes, 88; bleeding, 87; drum, 87;
    emergency, 89,104; failure, 87-89; fluid, 87-88, 102;
    hydraulic system (illus.), 89; leaking cylinder, 87-88;
    typical system (illus.), 88

Camping rules, 148-50
Carburetor, 42-43; floats, 44-45
CB radio, 130
Chain, 109
Choke baffle, 43-44
Clutch: adjustment, 102; broken, 100; failure to disengage,
    104; hydraulic linkage adjustment (illus.), 103
Condenser failure, symptoms of, 36-37
Cooling system, 74; dirty coolant, 72; fluid loss, 72; temperature
    gauge, 73
CPR (cardiopulmonary resuscitation), 115
CV (constant velocity) joints, 101

Distributor: cap, inspecting for problems (illus.), 24; loose, 27;
    contact point (illus.), 28
Drive shaft, 98; failure and removal, 101-2
Driving: across rivers, 110; following tire tracks, 111; in mud,
    109-10; safety, 5,160-61; without brakes, 89. *See also* ORVs

EGR (emmission gas recirculation) valve, 81
Emergency road gear, 10
Engine: basic principles, 9; basic parts, 6-7; cooling, 78; flooding,
    43-45; grinding noises, 61; hot smell, 75; lubricant, 13;
    maintenance, 82; oil leaks, 83; oil pressure, 76, 83-84; spare
    parts, 15-16; typical compartment (illus.), 8; used parts, 15
Environment, preservation of, 5, 107, 146-52. *See also* Noise
    pollution; Motorcycles; Off-road; Wilderness Act
Epoxy glue: for radiator repairs,74; for punctures, 85
Exposure. *See* Frostbite; Heat exhaustion; Hypothermia; Sunstroke
External voltage regulator, 67-68

Fan: auxiliary electric, 76; belt, 66, 76
First aid courses, 6. *See also* Safety
Flash floods, 113-14; 143
Flat tires: changing, 93-96; repairing, 90-93. *See also* Jacks; Tires
Flooded engine, 43-45
Flywheel, teeth worn, 61-62

Frostbite, symptoms and treatment, 120
Fuel system, 41-42; cold-start injector, 43; electric fuel pump, 46; emergency (illus.), 48; fuel flow test, 45; gas tank, 49; injection systems, 42-43; line blocked, 50; plugged fuel filter, 47; pump, 48-49; regaining fuel flow, 46-50; typical (illus.), 42; unfiltered fuel, 47; vapor lock, 46
Fuses, 55-56; bypassing, 56; replacing, 70
Fusible links, 66

Gasket leaks, 84
General Motors (GM) V-8 vehicles
Ground tackle, 108-109

Halyard, 109
Heat exhaustion, symptoms and treatment, 115-16
Hypothermia, 116, 119, 140-41; symptoms, 117-18; treatment, 118

Idle speed, 40
Ignition: air gap adjustments, 32-33; breakerless, 29-31; coil test (illus.), 22, 37; condenser failure, 36-37; confirming current to coil, 31; corroded wire ends, 24; diagnosis, 23; dirty points, 27; electronic, 53; failed components, 32; failure chart (illus.), 19; high energy system (HEI), 21; poor wire connection or short, 34; problems, 24-26; static timing (illus.), 39; switch, 57; testing points, 35-36; testing, 20-23; timing, 27, 38-41, 69; typical system (illus.), 21
Insect stings. *See* Bee stings; Yellow jackets
Intake manifold leaks, 80-81

Jacks, 93-96; bumper vs. hydraulic, 93-94; high-lift, 114; makeshift log (illus.), 95; safe jacking technique (illus.), 93; safety, 93-95
John Muir Publications, Inc., 4

Lubrication system, typical (illus.), 84

Manual transmission: failure, 100-1; gearboxes, 100
Maps: approved off-road trails, 4, 147; topographical contours (illus.), 132; reading topographical, 133; U.S. Forest Service, 4; U.S. Geological Survey, 4
Master cylinder, 102
Mechanical knowledge, 4
Motor oil, 13, 76. *See also* Oil
Motorcycles: best for off-road, 152; impact on trails,150-52; motocross, 151-52

Noise pollution, 149-50
Noises: "clunk" sounds, 97; engine grinding, 61, 98; screeching, 101; starter chatter, 60; whistling sounds, 81

Off-road: conditions, 107; conservation, 107, 113, 146-52; driving, 110-13; equipment, 13; flash floods, 113-14; getting unstuck, 13, 107, 111-13; trash, 149. *See also* ORVs; Safety
Oil: consumption, 85; pan punctures, 84-86; pressure, 76, 83-84; pump failure, 86. *See also* Motor oil
ORVs (Off-Road Vehicles): automatic transmission, 98; dirt bikes, 150-52; fuel-injected, 43; getting unstuck, 13, 107, 111-13; ground tackle, 13; maintenance, 4; manual transmission, 100-1; miscellaneous supplies, 12; pushstarting, 53; repair manuals, 4; safety gear, 10; safety precautions, 3, 5, 160-1; supplies, 13; temporary repairs, 4-5; Toyota pickups, 4. *See also* Driving; Flat tires; Motorcycles; Off-road

Poisonous bites. *See* Bee stings; Snakebite; Yellow jackets
Radiator: leaks and punctures, 72-74; removing cap, 72
Radio, as "homing device," 57. *See also* CB radio
Red Cross, 6
Regulator, testing, 68
Repairs: diagnosis, 6-9, 20; emergency, 8; tools, 9-10; supplies, 9-10
Rotor maladies (illus.), 25
RPMs, 78, 111

Safety: gear, 10; provisions, 14-15; in dangerous terrain, 5. *See also* Driving; Survival
Shelter, using vehicle as, 139-41
Shim, makeshift, 62
Silicone sealant, 49, 99
Slave cylinder, 102
Snakebite, 120-25; avoiding, 124-25; symptoms and treatment, 122-24
Snakes, 51, 88, 124-25; copperhead, 121; coral, 121; rattlesnakes,121; water moccasin,121
Spare parts,15-16; checklist,16
Spark plugs, 23; grounding wires, 21-22
SSB/VHF radios, 131
Starter, 53-55; cleaning, 63; faulty motor, 63; faulty solenoid, 60; faulty solenoid, starting (illus.), 58; relay, 53-55; solenoid, 53-54; spins free, 59; testing, 54
Steering, loss of, 104
Sunstroke, symptoms and treatment, 116
Survival: attracting help, 130-31, 133, 141; building a fire, 141; in cold weather, 118, 140-41; in the desert, 129, 133, 139, 141-42; finding water, 135-39; gear, 13-15, 135; going for help, 131-32; international emergency signals (illus.), 134; proper clothing for, 143-45; shelter, 139-43; skills, 5-6; sleeping bags, 145; staying dry, 143-44; water requirements, 129, 135-36. *See also* Safety; Shelter; Water

Temperature gauge, 73; faulty, 77-79
Thermostat, stuck, 79-80
Thermostatic switch, 76
Timing. *See* Ignition
Timing advance mechanism, 71
Tire surface, 111-12
Tires: blocking, 94; inflator and sealor, 112; jacks, 93-96; offroad, 92; oversized, 107; puncture repair kit, 90-91; temporary repairs, 92-93; torn valve stems, 92-93; traction for, 112. *See also* Flat tires; Jacks
Tools: emergency, 10; storage, 11
Tree protector, 112-13

U.S. Forest Service, 3-4, 107, 129
Universal joints, 97-98

Voltage regulator, 65

Water: as emergency brake fluid, 88; disinfecting, 137; finding, 135-39; *Giardia lamblia*, 137; solar still, 137-39; for survival, 72
Wilderness Act, 147
Wildlife conservation, 148-49
Winch, 107; bumper-mounted, 109; cable safety, 112; hooking up, 112-13; lever (come-along), 108-9; right size, 108; tree protector, 112-13

Yellow jacket (wasp), 127

Other Books from John Muir Publications

22 Days Series
These pocket-size itineraries are a refreshing departure from ordinary guide-books. Each author has an in-depth knowledge of the region covered and offers 22 tested daily itineraries through their favorite destinations. Included are not only "must see" attractions but also little-known villages and hidden "jewels" as well as valuable general information.

22 Days Around the World by R. Rapoport and B. Willes (65-31-9)
22 Days in Alaska by Pamela Lanier (28-68-0)
22 Days in the American Southwest by R. Harris (28-88-5)
22 Days in Asia by R. Rapoport and B. Willes (65-17-3)
22 Days in Australia by John Gottberg (65-40-8)
22 Days in California by Roger Rapoport (28-93-1)
22 Days in China by Gaylon Duke and Zenia Victor (28-72-9)
22 Days in Dixie by Richard Polese (65-18-1)
22 Days in Europe by Rick Steves (65-05-X)
22 Days in Florida by Richard Harris (65-27-0)
22 Days in France by Rick Steves (65-07-6)
22 Days in Germany, Austria & Switzerland by R. Steves (65-39-4)
22 Days in Great Britain by Rick Steves (65-38-6)
22 Days in Hawaii by Arnold Schuchter (28-92-3)
22 Days in India by Anurag Mathur (28-87-7)
22 Days in Japan by David Old (28-73-7)
22 Days in Mexico by S. Rogers and T. Rosa (65-41-6)
22 Days in New England by Anne Wright (28-96-6)
22 Days in New Zealand by Arnold Schuchter (28-86-9)
22 Days in Norway, Denmark & Sweden by R. Steves (28-83-4)
22 Days in the Pacific Northwest by R. Harris (28-97-4)
22 Days in Spain & Portugal by Rick Steves (65-06-8)
22 Days in the West Indies by C. & S. Morreale (28-74-5)
All 22 Days titles are 128 to 152 pp. and $7.95 each, except 22 Days Around the World, which is 192 pp. and $9.95.

"Kidding Around" Travel Guides for Children
Written for kids eight years of age and older. Generously illustrated in two colors with imaginative characters and images. An adventure to read and a treasure to keep.
Kidding Around Atlanta, Anne Pedersen (65-35-1) 64 pp. $9.95
Kidding Around London, Sarah Lovett (65-24-6) 64 pp. $9.95
Kidding Around Los Angeles (65-34-3) 64 pp. $9.95
Kidding Around New York City, Sarah Lovett (65-33-5) 64 pp. $9.95
Kidding Around San Francisco, Rosemary Zibart (65-23-8) 64 pp. $9.95
Kidding Around Washington, D.C., Anne Pedersen (65-25-4) 64 pp. $9.95

Asia Through the Back Door, Rick Steves and John Gottberg (28-76-1) 336 pp. $13.95

Buddhist America: Centers, Retreats, Practices, Don Morreale (28-94-X) 400 pp. $12.95

Bus Touring: Charter Vacations, U.S.A., Stuart Warren (28-95-8) 168 pp. $9.95

Catholic America: Self-Renewal Centers and Retreats, Patricia Christian-Meyer (65-20-3) 325 pp. $13.95

Choices & Changes: Preparing for Pregnancy and Parenthood, Brenda E. Aikey-Keller (65-44-0) 256 pp. $13.95

Complete Guide to Bed & Breakfasts, Inns & Guesthouses, 1989-90 Edition, Pamela Lanier (65-09-2) 520 pp. $14.95

Elderhostels: The Students' Choice, Mildred Hyman (65-28-9) 224 pp. $12.95

Europe 101: History & Art for the Traveler, Rick Steves and Gene Openshaw (28-78-8) 372 pp. $12.95

Europe Through the Back Door, Rick Steves (28-84-2) 404 pp. $12.95

Floating Vacations: River, Lake, and Ocean Adventures, Michael White (65-32-7) 256 pp. $17.95

Gypsying After 40: A Guide to Adventure and Self-Discovery, Bob Harris (28-71-0) 264 pp. $12.95

The Heart of Jerusalem, Arlynn Nellhaus (28-79-6) 312 pp. $12.95

Indian America: A Traveler's Companion, Eagle/Walking Turtle (65-29-7) 336 pp. $14.95

Mona Winks: Self-Guided Tours of Europe's Top Museums, Rick Steves (28-85-0) 450 pp. $14.95

The On and Off the Road Cookbook, Carl Franz (28-27-3) 272 pp. $8.50

The People's Guide to Mexico, Carl Franz (28-99-0) 608 pp. $15.95

The People's Guide to RV Camping in Mexico, Carl Franz with Steve Rogers (28-91-5) 256 pp. $13.95

Ranch Vacations: The Complete Guide to Guest, Fly-Fishing, and Cross-Country Skiing Ranches, Eugene Kilgore (65-30-0) 256 pp. $17.95

The Shopper's Guide to Mexico, Steve Rogers and Tina Rosa (28-90-7) 224 pp. $9.95

Ski Tech's Guide to Equipment, Skiwear, and Accessories, edited by Bill Tanler (65-45-9) 200 pp. $14.95

Ski Tech's Guide to Maintenance and Repair, edited by Bill Tanler (65-46-7) 200 pp. $14.95

Traveler's Guide to Asian Culture, Kevin Chambers (65-14-9) 356 pp. $13.95

Traveler's Guide to Healing Centers and Retreats in North America, Martine Rudee and Jonathan Blease (65-15-7) 240 pp. $11.95

Undiscovered Islands of the Caribbean, Burl Willes (28-80-X) 216 pp. $12.95

Automotive Repair Manuals

Each JMP automotive manual gives clear step-by-step instructions together with illustrations that show exactly how each system in the vehicle comes apart and goes back together. They tell everything a novice or experienced mechanic needs to know to perform periodic maintenance, tuneups, troubleshooting, and repair of the brake, fuel and emission control, electrical, cooling, clutch, transmission, driveline, steering, and suspension systems and even rebuild the engine.

How to Keep Your VW Alive (65-12-2) 424 pp. $17.95
How to Keep Your Golf/Jetta/Rabbit/Scirocco Alive (65-21-1) 420 pp. $17.95
How to Keep Your Honda Car Alive (28-55-9) 272 pp. $17.95
How to Keep Your Subaru Alive (65-11-4) 480 pp. $17.95
How to Keep Your Toyota Pickup Alive (28-81-3) 392 pp. $17.95
How to Keep Your Datsun/Nissan Alive (28-65-6) 544 pp. $17.95

Other Automotive Books

The Greaseless Guide to Car Care Confidence: Take the Terror Out of Talking to Your Mechanic, Mary Jackson (65-19-X) 224 pp. $14.95

Off-Road Emergency Repair & Survival, James Ristow (65-26-2) 160 pp. $9.95

Road & Track's Used Car Classics, edited by Peter Bohr (28-69-9) 272 pp. $12.95

Ordering Information

If you cannot find our books in your local bookstore, you can order directly from us. Your books will be sent to you via UPS (for U.S. destinations), and you will receive them approximately 10 days from the time that we receive your order. Include $2.75 for the first item ordered and $.50 for each additional item to cover shipping and handling costs. UPS shipments to post office boxes take longer to arrive; if possible, please give us a street address. For airmail within the U.S., enclose $4.00 per book for shipping and handling. All foreign orders will be shipped surface rate. Please enclose $3.00 for the first item and $1.00 for each additional item. Please inquire for airmail rates.

Method of Payment

Your order may be paid by check, money order, or credit card. We cannot be responsible for cash sent through the mail. All payments must be made in U.S. dollars drawn on a U.S. bank. Canadian postal money orders in U.S. dollars are also acceptable. For VISA, MasterCard, or American Express orders, include your card number, expiration date, and your signature, or call (505)982-4078. Books ordered on American Express cards can be shipped only to the billing address of the cardholder. Sorry, no C.O.D.'s. Residents of sunny New Mexico, add 5.625% tax to the total.

Address all orders and inquiries to:
John Muir Publications
P.O. Box 613
Santa Fe, NM 87504
(505)982-4078